The Hedgehog Diaries

The Hedgehog Diaries

*A Story of Faith,
Hope and Bristle*

SARAH SANDS

With illustrations by Evie Dunne

Every effort has been made to contact copyright holders of material reproduced in this book. We would be pleased to rectify any omissions in subsequent editions. Please contact the pubisher at info@newriverbooks.co.uk.

Published in 2023 by New River Books.
www.newriverbooks.co.uk

10 9 8 7 6 5 4 3 2 1

Copyright © Sarah Sands 2023

Sarah Sands has asserted her right under the Copyright, Designs and Patents Act 1988 to be identified as the author of this work. All rights reserved. No part of this publication may be reproduced, stored in a retrieval system or transmitted in any form, or by any means (electronic, mechanical, or otherwise) without the prior written permission of both the copyright owners and the publisher.

Illustrations copyright © Evie Dunne 2023

A CIP catalogue record for this book is available from the British Library.

ISBN: 978-1-915780-02-7

Printed and bound by CPI (UK) Ltd, Croydon CR0 4YY
Cover design: Two Associates

In memory of my father, Noel Harvey,
who loved the natural world

CONTENTS

1. On finding a hedgehog
2. The world according to hedgehogs
3. Winter: in sickness and in health
4. Mrs Tiggy-Winkle and the poetry of hedgehogs
5. Prehistoric hedgehogs and dusking
6. The release of Peggy
7. Communities of hedgehogs – Kirtlington and Shropshire
8. Grief, faith, hope and hedgehogs
9. Hibernation, sleep and blonde bombshells
10. Friends and enemies: badgers, dogs and humans
11. War and peace

1

ON FINDING A HEDGEHOG

On a damp, mulchy October afternoon, my two-year-old grandson spotted a dark, round shape caught in a piece of netting by our pond.

"What is it, thing?" he asked in newly minted vocabulary. He has come to recognise mice, voles, deer and foxes but this creature made his eyes widen. It was sui generis. It was a hedgehog. We tried gently to shake it free, but it gave only the smallest tremor. It did not seem well. I told my grandson not to touch it because it was prickly, and my husband fetched a box for it. "Poke it, ouch," said my grandson. We named it Horace.

My husband is the son of a Yorkshire vet, and notably unsentimental about animals. Unusually, for a couple in their sixties living partly in the countryside post-lockdown, we do not have a dog. Sometimes dog walkers treat us with sideways sympathy, reassuring us that their liquid-eyed pets will not threaten us. Other times, they confront us directly with their suspicions: "Where is your dog?"

I am also running out of time for my life ambition to ride a horse across Norfolk beaches. The only riding that I have managed this year is in the children's sitting trot class that I've joined, my shire horse plodding deferentially behind their Shetland ponies.

Yet, something melted within my husband when confronted with the hedgehog. What was it? Something of Tolkien about a creature from somewhere else, finding itself in danger. Something sturdy and good-natured but in peril.

Ted Hughes described his response to finding a hedgehog in a letter to a friend:

> ...heard a commotion in the hedge, and after a while, out trundled a hedgehog, merry as you like, and obviously out for a good time. I thought he might make a jolly companion for an evening so I brought him in. After a while I noticed he had disappeared and later heard a noise just like the sobbing of a little child, but very faint, and it continued

for long enough. I traced it to the pile of boxes, and there was my comrade, with his nose pressed in a corner in a pool of tears and his face all wet, and snivelling and snuffling his heart out. I could have kissed him for compassion. I don't know why I'm so sympathetic towards hedgehogs.

The sound of hedgehogs is what seems to capture most completely the human heart – they can squeak, chirp, huff, puff, hiss and sing, although a friend who came across mating hedgehogs (how hedgehogs mate is one of the great questions of scientific and civil endeavour) said it was like stumbling across some pagan, orgiastic ritual.

Our small hedgehog made no noise. Kim lifted it in cupped hands and placed it in a cardboard box while I put out some milk and bread. There are three basic mistakes in that sentence alone, but we had much to learn about hedgehogs.

Then, ancestry kicked in. For my husband, a generation, and for the hedgehog, millions of years of survival. Kim tried to judge the temperature between hibernation and untimely awakening and moved the box nearer the Aga. Then he took a comb and a jug of warm, salty water and tenderly cleared the flies from the hedgehog's eyes. My grandson watched, from a wary distance, camouflaged by his anorak and wellington boots. He carried a twig, hopeful of using it as a kind of defibrillator. "Poke it, now? Horace, hedgehog?"

Kim shook his head and said in a low, surgeon's voice: "I fear we may be losing him."

He stood up, frowned and looked at his phone. It was moving towards dusk, a slice of white light compressed within a gun-grey sky. The trees were losing their leaves after some high winds during the week. Only the tartan-coloured greens and reds of the pair of crab apple trees given to us by my father remained doughty. The landscape was shivering. This should have been the time of day, though not the season, when the hedgehog would be readying itself for a surprisingly brisk walk towards the line of small hawthorn and rose bushes we had planted.

Unwittingly, we had been creating the right conditions for hedgehogs. When we moved to this home a decade ago, we had torn up the tennis court in favour of a wildflower patch. We had planted beech hedges and rows of fruit trees. We had created a swimming pond, with shallow water for reeds and lilies. We are in East Anglia, with its big, open arable fields, which are no places for hedgehogs. But in our patch of grassy paths, fruit trees, brambles and beds of leaves, we had been unknowingly courting hedgehogs. And then when one trundled out, merry as you like, we had left a death trap for it with a pond-clearing net on a pole.

My husband made a call. Then he picked up the box and took it to the car. He said that he was taking Horace to hospital.

I laughed. There was no such thing as a hedgehog hospital, certainly nobody would take a hedgehog on a Sunday evening; the best thing would be to leave the hedgehog overnight and see how it was in the morning. There are three major mistakes in that sentence too.

There *was* a hedgehog hospital, which turned out to be part of a network of hedgehog carers, foster parents, campaigners and policy makers. Anyone with any experience of hedgehogs would know that if one is ill, you must act fast to save it. A small hedgehog wandering around at this time of year is likely to come from a late litter and lack resilience.

Discovering that a free, structured system of hedgehog social care exists in the UK – no hedgehog will be turned away – made me realise how deeply hedgehogs must be embedded in our culture, our literature, our history and psyche. Nowhere else in the world has quite the same relationship with hedgehogs. The British Hedgehog Preservation Society, whose patrons eclectically include Dame Twiggy and Ann Widdecombe, measures societal progress through the prism of hedgehog friendliness.

There are Hedgehog Street signs, hierarchies of university campuses based on outreach and access – for hedgehogs. There is a hedgehog-friendly football league. And there are cute videos of Mrs Tiggy-Winkle's nest building.

Our first call was Emma's Hedgehog Hotel, which is also Emma's home, down a farm track on the outskirts of King's Lynn. The medical triumphs and tragedies are detailed on Facebook, Instagram, Google, Amazon and Paypal. The hedgehog community is global and active.

My husband raced over and reported back via email. "She [Horace] is only four to six weeks old. Emma said I had done a terrific job in removing so many of the fly eggs, but she has a little trouble downstairs, where some have hatched into maggots and are exploring. So I am standing there with Emma as she gets her partner, big guns, vivid tats, to pick off the maggots with tweezers and she flushes the hedgehog's 'vagina' [said several times] with warm saline solution. She's now christened Peggy because Emma says every Hattie she has had has died on her, and I shall be watching her progress – be it long or short – on Instagram."

The following day a cheery text came from Emma: "Thank you for bringing her to me. She's lost a little weight overnight which is expected after all that flushing. Just hope all were removed [two praying emojis] for a gain tomorrow, Best wishes, Emma."

My husband was both ironic and intensely invested in Peggy's recovery. The charts of patients' weight gains were studied; Peggy seemed to be lagging behind. I later learned the official term for her condition: vaginal flystrike.

I was preoccupied elsewhere. Earlier in that autumn of 2021, my 92-year-old father had suffered major heart failure and he was now in hospital. I went to his house to fetch some things for him. There was his favourite armchair and beside it a side table: on it were his reading glasses, his folded copy of *The Times*, his piles of books about birds or classical music or the Church and his binoculars. A summary of him, really. Old-style Radio 4.

The chair looked starkly empty without his imprinted form, for he had always sprung up as I let myself into their bungalow: "Hello, darling, how lovely to see you."

He had risen more unsteadily of late and he touched the walls as he walked but I had not thought too much of it. He had also taken to wearing a scarf, which I thought sensible for his age, but turned out to be his modest precaution against a rattling in his chest.

Every Sunday, he would come to lunch with us, and it was when he phoned to say that on this occasion he might stay quietly at home that I had become alarmed. Was it his chest? I took him to A and E, and with little fuss and much gratitude, he saw a doctor, took some more pills and returned home. He thought he would sleep better that night. Two days later, he collapsed, suffering from heart failure and pneumonia. None of us was prepared for this moment of reckoning, for John Donne's line from "Memento Mori": "I dare not move my dim eyes any way/Despair behind and death before doth cast Such Terror."

He spent a week in hospital. Covid rules forbade visitors, so I would leave little notes for him each day, along with a copy of *The Times*. What news could I bring him? The fate of a hedgehog seemed about right, not too serious, not too taxing, a story of recovery.

Message from Emma: "She's had a couple of days of losses. Started wormer treatment on 19. Last two days overall gain of 15g [applause emojis]."

Meanwhile, the news on the Facebook page for her hedgehog hotel was motivational.

"Day 3 of Bertie's physiotherapy baths and what a lovely way to end the day. Today has been really hard [a line of broken heart emojis and a line of tearful face emojis]" I really needed to see his beautiful face and witness his strength and determination this evening.

"PS. If you ever get the chance to eradicate one living thing… press the button @flies. Goodbye today and I welcome a new day tomorrow.

"#hedgehog rescue,#sometimessouldestroying #welcomethenewday #whatdoesntbreakyoumakesyoustronger #wishIhadamagicwand."

My dad was not faring so well. The hospital was at full stretch. A doctor did phone to explain that the heart could be managed through drugs but nothing more could be done. Another doctor showed me with a gesture of hands pumping an accordion in and out. This was how a heart moves. Then he demonstrated how a heart moved after failure. Barely at all. If my grandson were looking at it, he would wield his stick to look for movement.

They were keeping him in for further tests. Blood in the urine. Fluid on the lungs. They had asked him if he would consent to a Do Not Resuscitate sign at the end of his bed. Not so fast. Dad wanted to survive. He shook his head: No, no, no. His fight for life was now a matter of will.

Nearly eight years ago, my father had a heart operation at Papworth and they told him that it would extend his life by five years. We are all on borrowed time but my dad's heart was three years past its sell-by-date.

I searched for him back then in the ICU, behind a curtain, wired up and breathless. There would be an end to beeping and bright lights, I told him. There would be Beethoven and birdsong again. We would release him back into the world. I didn't know if I could keep the same promise this time.

The pounds of flesh he owed to fate were falling away, his checked shirt flapping on him, his trousers roomy.

I started to hear from doctors, including my own cousin, a form of words chosen by medics to pave the way for bereavement without sounding too brutally sudden: "It could be weeks, or months." We were entering the darkest valley.

I thought of the words of the philosopher Roger Scruton: "Love is a relationship between dying things." Everything about my dad, a shadow of himself, seemed newly vivid. His white hair and boyish eagerness, his tropes, his scarves, his kindly essence. His friend, the local vicar, said of my dad that his prevailing characteristic was humility. This turned out to be his great survival mechanism.

We decided to move him to a nursing home, so that we would be allowed to see him. If he stayed at the hospital he would almost certainly die alone, in a cacophony of Covid emergency. I googled local homes and spoke to one run by a former nurse with a patient, practical matter. Once he was booked in, my sister and I drove to the hospital to collect him. His weight had plummeted again and he was sitting dressed but hollow-eyed and unshaven in a wheelchair. A week is a long time in hospital.

A nurse on double shift because of staff shortages helped us get him into the car. Along with many others, I had learned the lesson of the pandemic: the quality of compassion.

"Am I going home?" asked my father. I had no certain answers, no promises. We both talked of the spring, as a metaphor for hope. And to fill the truthful silences, we talked about Peggy's amazing recovery. Emma had messaged to say that she had gained weight and was on her way to a foster parent. Joined-up social care. Our daughter sent a gif of a hedgehog in the back of a car wearing a seat belt.

Sometimes it is just easier to talk about hedgehogs. For one friend of mine, they were her means of anaesthetising the pain of human suffering and being closer to the son whom she loved and lost. Jane, whom I will feature with the depth she deserves in a later chapter, lost her teenage boy to meningitis while he was on holiday with friends. One moment Felix was playing cricket on the lawn, the next feeling a little unwell, then sick beyond treatment. Jane, along with her husband Justin, created a legacy of compassion by bringing excess food, otherwise thrown out by supermarkets and restaurants, to those in need. You might have seen the bright-green vans with their Felix logo driven around London by volunteers.

But in the immediate aftermath of Felix's death, Jane could not think about legacy. His death was so sudden and unimaginable that she was derailed. Nothing made sense. The usual patterns and pleasures of life had no meaning. After several months of pitch darkness, Jane found a cause that her eggshell state of mind could cope with. She could not work, she could not bear society, but she could care about hedgehogs. Because Felix did.

She came to see me when I was the editor of the *Evening Standard* to talk about a plan for creating hedgehog highways. I remember admiring her courage in minding about anything at all. She was accompanied by an expert called Hugh Warwick, who seemed nice enough. I did not realise at the time that I was talking to the David Attenborough of the hedgehog world.

On an October afternoon, I found a hedgehog, and came to glimpse a hedgehog community, a system of social care, a passionate fringe of volunteers gingerly regarded by the more mainstream hedgehog environmentalists. And I discovered that poets and philosophers, people of faith and those at war have turned to the hedgehog as a symbol of innocence, mystery, political purpose, courage, peace and equilibrium.

The Hedgehog Diaries

I understood why saving Peggy became important to me when I read Philip Larkin's poem "The Mower".

A mower stalled, twice: kneeling, I found
A hedgehog, jammed up against the blades.
Killed. It had been in the long grass.

I had seen it before, and even fed it once.
Now I had mauled its unobtrusive world
Unmendably. Burial was no help.

Next morning I got up and it did not.
The first days after a death, the new absence
Is always the same: we should be careful
Of each other, we should be kind
While there is still time.

This book is dedicated to all those who love hedgehogs. It is also dedicated to my father, who continued to lose weight during the winter and whom we fought to keep until the spring.

2

THE WORLD ACCORDING TO HEDGEHOGS

The pandemic was hard for humans. It stress tested leadership, logistics, community, globalism. It raised the question of how we should live, and for whom and for what.

Hedgehogs fared better, partly because they are not social animals like us. They are nocturnal, and rely on scent and to a lesser extent hearing as a way of interpreting life. Unlike badgers, who are family minded, hedgehogs do not seek company, even of their own kind. Mating is an ingenious theatrical aberration with no follow-up companionship. It's all just keep calm and carry on.

The first person to discern the life skills of the hedgehog was, it seems, the ancient Greek poet Archilochus. "The fox knows many things," he wrote, "but the hedgehog knows one big thing."

Two thousand years later, in a celebrated essay on foxes and hedgehogs, Isaiah Berlin explained the philosophical significance. "There exists a great chasm between those, one side, who relate everything to a single central vision, one system, less or more coherent or articulate in terms of which they understand, think and feel – a single, universal organising principle in terms of which alone all that they are and say has significance – and, on the other side, those who pursue many ends, often unrelated and even contradictory, connected, if at all, only in some de facto way, for some psychological or physiological cause, related by no moral or aesthetic principle."

He took as his study Tolstoy, who wanted very much to be a hedgehog, although his artistry led him towards the fox. "Tolstoy perceived reality in its multiplicity as a collection of separate entities round and into which he saw with a clarity and penetration scarcely ever equalled, but he believed only in one unitary whole."

Tolstoy preached "simplicity of life and purity of purpose" and wanted to prove a unified vision beyond individual experience. He talked of the root of the tree rather than the leaves. (What is wrong with leaves? Much more interesting for hedgehogs).

His belief in scientific enquiry led him to envision history as the sum of verifiable human experience; but also to question: whose history?

The heroic view of history overvalues power when much of what makes our lives better we owe to people who do not seek glory. The pandemic was the case in point. Our eyes were opened to those who kept the country running rather than those who ran the country. The stirrings of the trade union movement, rights for workers, or rather working-from-homers, is a nod to Tolstoy. One can live by the wisdom of the hedgehog, and institutions have been created out of it.

Berlin writes: "Those who went about their ordinary business without feeling heroic emotions or thinking that they were actors upon the well-lighted stage of history were the most useful to their country and community while those who tried to grasp the general course of events and wanted to take part in history... were the most useless."

As a career journalist, I have closely followed the cut and thrust of politics. My period of closest observation was as editor of Radio 4's *Today* programme, during Brexit. It was a time of political existentialism. One Conservative politician who stood in the leadership contest during this time was Rory Stewart, the adventurer, writer and diplomat. He has spoken in the House of Commons with passion and breadth about foreign and security policy and the nature of democracy. But his most watched speech on YouTube was the one he made in November 2015, about hedgehogs.

After quoting Archilochus' proposition, Stewart noted that it was the first time that Parliament had discussed hedgehogs since 1566, in relation to a bounty for the collection for them, as they were then considered vermin.

Stewart appealed to pre-history: "The hedgehog, and its ancestor, narrowly missed being crushed under the foot of Tyrannosaurus Rex. The hedgehog was around long before the human species: it existed 56 million years ago. It tells us a great deal about British civilisation…"

He also pronounced it "an environmental indicator" and a lesson in "scientific humility – the hedgehog has after all of course been studied for over 2000 years."

He ended with Thomas Hardy:

When the hedgehog travels furtively over
                the lawn,
One may say, "He strove that such innocent
                creatures should come to no harm
But he could do little for them; and now
                he is gone.
If, when hearing that I have been stilled at last,
                they stand at the door,
Watching the full-starred heavens that
                winter sees,
Will this thought rise on those who will meet my
                face no more,
"He was one who had an eye for such mysteries?"

The touchingly potent silhouette of the hedgehog, making his journey. Rory Stewart is someone who understands the nature of journeys, having once walked across Afghanistan, Iran, Pakistan and Nepal: walking as a sign of peace in areas of potential conflict. It was a soft echo of Gandhi's political walks in search of truth and wisdom.

Rory Stewart has now left politics. In a decade of speeches, I ask him, why does he think this ode to the hedgehog is the one that everyone remembers?

Well, he says, it is because there is something magically appealing about hedgehogs. And in a political world so fractious and binary, it is a subject on which everyone can soften and converse and be human.

He notes that if you wish to avoid the sound and fury of social media, you will always be safe discussing hedgehogs. Nobody is going to tear you down. This is broadly true, though I come to discover that identity politics is starting to threaten the hedgehog community, creating culture wars between scientists and carers.

There is something else. Rory says the setting of small, spiky creatures in the epic frame of time and philosophy is poignant. Isn't this how we see ourselves? We are not grand in the scheme of things but we are doughty. And it makes sense to stick together. While climate change caused by humans threatens the seasonal rhythms of hedgehogs, it is humans – the age of the Anthropocene – who may not survive the evolution of the planet.

It is Tolkien again. Something emerges from the wild

into a safe boundary of a garden. We welcome it but must also help it on its way, by leaving a bowl of food and water and creating a tunnel into the next garden or open land so that it can continue its journey. And if it is sick, it is our responsibility.

New message from Emma, saying that Peggy is up to 896g, having gained 45g overnight. After she has been to her foster parent for overwintering, she can return to us in the spring. Emma will send a list of criteria for suitability for a patron's garden.

Ha! Our perverse lack of a dog is at last a competitive advantage. I send some estate-agent-style pictures of the garden, basically leaves and bramble. I take a side shot of the pond to make it look shallower and put the ramps centre stage. I wait to hear.

Text from Emma: "Looks great. Just walking dogs."

Meanwhile, hedgehogs do seem to insert themselves into history. We discuss Downing Street parties against a drum beat of war. My local MP in Norfolk is Liz Truss; she'salso Foreign Secretary. I listen to her on the *Today* programme warning that Britain stands for freedom and will defend the free democracy of Ukraine as part of Nato against the aggressive stance of Russia.

The hedgehog is a symbol of NATO, naked chest puffed out, on the march, with its back bristling. It is said to embody the spirit and determination of Allies to defend themselves against aggressors. Why? Because it is a peaceful creature that bristles when attacked. Its counterforce against, for instance, snakes is formidable. But it stands no chance against badgers, and the hideousness of that death we will address later. Thank goodness the symbol for Russia is a sickle rather than a badger, which would disembowel the Nato hedgehog. The Danish Atlantic Association used the hedgehog symbol as a rebuke to the Danish communists' dove. Hedgehogs are not belligerent but they will fight.

It was General Eisenhower, in 1951, who urged European countries to adopt a "hedgehog" defence to slow down enemy forces. This is perhaps the quagmire which Europe warns Russia will be the consequence of enemy action. It also speaks to a quiet stubbornness on the part of the British people. Boris Johnson, then Prime Minister, alluded thus to our defensive alliance against Moscow: "We need to make the quills of the porcupine indigestible."

My Instagram feed is now 70 per cent hedgehog, the glistening snouts in bowls a reminder that while the rest of the country diets in January, hedgehog social care is all about weight gain. Emma's hedgehog hotel reports in on Phoebe. "[Jazz hands.] Phoebe has been treated for the usual internal parasites and has nearly completed her meds for ringworm. Phoebe now weighs 655g."

Emma's instagram followers have also been cheering on Paddy: "very weak little late autumn juvenile weighing only 269g. The poor little hog is riddled with the usual nasties. Despite fluids it's lost 28g overnight. It is drinking this morning independently which is a positive sign."

Update: "[crying emoji face] Sadly, Paddy has just passed."

The care home suggest that I find a new belt for my dad because there are not enough holes left in his current one to keep his trousers up. He is eating quite well so they are concerned that he cannot put on weight. I have been concentrating on fluids, finding that he especially likes Cambridgeshire apple juice made from Discoveries and Coxes. The nurse on duty phones to say no more apple juice. The acid is having a destructive effect. Water only.

I wish it were spring and I could take him outside to feel the air on his face and hear the birds. It is surely a hedgehog philosophy that freedom is dignity.

I am also concerned about how much I can visit. The pandemic is coming to an end and we are returning to our offices. The working from home was a vote for hands over heads, when caring for families became part of the day.

Philosophical question: what is a life well lived? Is it a balance of private and professional or are we aiming for the obituary? Should a good life encourage us to be more like hedgehogs? I turn to holy wisdom, the former Archbishop of Canterbury, Rowan Williams. One of his *Desert Island Discs* choices was "The Hedgehog's Song" by the Incredible String Band. It is a charming ballad about an unsuccessful lover and the intervention of a "funny little hedgehog" who divines that he has "never quite learned the song" – presumably missing a central truth. (There aren't many famous hedgehog songs, and on mention of *Desert Island Discs*, Dr Williams chuckles, recalling how his staff feared that the BBC production team might accidentally fish out the wrong hedgehog song, the one by Terry Pratchett with its non-ecclesiastical lyric: "The hedgehog can never be buggered at all.")

I ask Dr Williams what it is that the hedgehog knows. What in his view is the universal truth that has escaped the skittish fox?

His response is hedgehog-centric. I should not perhaps be searching for universal truths. I should not be looking for grand solutions to the world's problems. I should be looking right in front of me.

What the hedgehog has is the capacity to focus on what is there, at that moment.

Dr Williams considers the matter a bit longer and then says: "I feel like the hedgehog's job is the next thing to be done."

It is methodical. It is sequential.

A little political context to our conversation. It is the start of February, described as a "meltdown in Downing Street". The Prime Minister, Boris Johnson, in defending himself against a police investigation into parties at Downing Street, misleadingly accuses the Labour leader Keir Starmer of failing to prosecute the child sex offender Jimmy Savile. The head of No 10's policy unit resigns in protest over Johnson's behaviour. It looks like a political tornado; the drama never lets up.

No wonder hedgehog behaviour, methodical, sequential, modest, seems appealing. Dr Williams is particularly taken by the word sequential. He says: "Sequential is a good word. It is a recognition that today you are constrained by what you did yesterday and your job today is to make something possible tomorrow."

The attentiveness to the here and now is at odds with the flamboyant initiatives beloved of politicians. Rowan Williams picks his words carefully. "The seduction of our culture and our political culture is solutions looking for problems. It is 'here is something exciting' but it doesn't put food on the table or unblock the drains."

The spiritual leader finds himself using the same expression as Boris Johnson's former adviser and now nemesis Dominic Cummings, who talks of "fixing the drains" by plotting the Prime Minister's removal. Dr Williams shudders at the "moral vulgarity" of our present leadership. "It is vulgarity in the sense of a debased currency of relationship, of what we owe to one another.

"Morality is partly about the messages you send one another; the message that certain kinds of people don't have to bother is a pretty bad one. It is corrosive to lack moral solidarity. I am sure that hedgehogs are much better at this."

What Dr Williams is looking for, however, is not Cummings-style creative destruction as a remedy but attention to detail. He says that he would like "a few more people in leadership who thought that their job was to solve more identifiable problems rather than change the world."

He talks admiringly of the First Minister of Wales, Mark Drakeford, as "utterly uncharismatic – that is one of the things I like about him".

Whether Drakeford is as enamoured of the description, I am not sure. But Dr Williams pronounces him a "rather hedgehog-like politician", with his qualities of patience and accuracy, so I am on board.

It is leadership itself that appears to have become overblown. Dr Williams seems to agree with Tolstoy that much valuable work goes unrecognised because it is not accompanied by fame or glory. He also says that something missed about Tolkien's work is that heroic acts are in the past or, if in the present, ineffectual. "The real work is being done elsewhere."

I think of Rory Stewart's description of the fate of hedgehogs, small and purposeful, set against the grandiosity of politics. And of the care home staff, playing board games with patients during lockdown to take their mind off the Covid death at the end of the corridor, confronting mortality with cups of tea and humming. It suddenly seems to me that the unheroic hedgehog could be the symbol of the pandemic. While leaders pontificated or partied, elsewhere, people drove the buses and set about vaccinating.

There are hedgehog/hobbit tasks for improving the world and there is a hedgehog-like state of mind. Dr Williams describes these as "prosaic virtues". "You appreciate the moments of enrichment and happiness but you don't expect it all to be like that. The bottom line is, 'here is a job to be done and it is up to me to do it.'"

Unfashionable virtues, celebrated in unfashionable Victorian hymns. Dr Williams particularly likes: "Awake my soul and with the sun, your daily stage of duty run…"

I tell him that some environmentalists believe that we will know nature is back in balance once the hedgehogs return in numbers. The hedgehogs are a sign of hope.

He chuckles: "That's a wonderful image, very counter-intuitive. You can say that the lion is coming to Narnia, but the hedgehog coming back to Narnia is much better.

"It is interesting that there are certain creatures, like hedgehogs and dolphins and otters, which speak to us about what is precarious and what is easily lost. When we see them we also understand that there is a backdrop to our lives; we are not just there on a spot-lit stage on our own."

Can hedgehogs provide a moral framework? The late Ronald Dworkin, philosopher and constitutional lawyer, thought so. You might think it odd that a legal scholar should turn his attention to hedgehogs, but there they are nevertheless, representing fundamental concepts. In his book *Justice for Hedgehogs*, he propounds a theory essentially at one with the Rowan Williams message that self-respect requires us also to respect others. Morality is found in our relationship with others. And when we look back on our life, our behaviour towards others determines the quality of it.

Dworkin writes: "The only value we can find in living

in the foothills of death, as we do, is adverbial value. We must find the value of living – the meaning of life – in living well, just as we find value in loving or painting or writing or singing or diving well. There is no other enduring value or meaning in our lives, but that is value and meaning enough. In fact it's wonderful."

If we mean to obey the commands of both ethics and morality, we must discover what happiness really is and what the virtues really demand.

Dworkin continues: "The hedgehogs' faith that all true values form an interlocking network, that each of our convictions about what is good or right or beautiful plays some role in supporting each of our other convictions in each of those domains of value. We can seek truth about morality only by pursuing coherence endorsed by conviction."

It is the hedgehog network of moral concepts and ethics that produces happiness. And, according to Dworkin, a just person must be happier than an unjust one.

Hedgehogs may be unaware of the moral principles invested in them. They are too busy worrying about maggots. But there is something about the creature's association with modesty, steadfastness and harming nobody that makes it a fitting role model. We get hedgehogs when there is a balance of nature, a co-existence with our environment rather than a domination or destruction of it. We find hedgehogs when we have paid our debts and put things right. And, on the Dworkin moral train of thought, hedgehogs are a sign of an examined life.

The Hedgehog Diaries

Rowan Williams describes the equilibrium of "welcoming" what life brings you, for good or for ill. He says that acceptance is a form of faith. I think of my father's animated pleasure in a joke about motorbikes, of which he knows nothing, with the care home cleaner, or news of one his grandchildren. His biblical joy, too deep for words, at touching the face of his new great-grandson at his bedside, even though he is too weak to hold the infant or indeed sit up any more. His earlier fretfulness has gone: here he is bedridden, pale, shaky and luminous with gratitude for human exchanges or just lying between sleep and wakefulness.

Gifts pile up unopened. After a lifetime of reading, he has put aside his books. He is quietly waiting.

I am still anxious to cram a little more entertainment into his life, to remind him of his formerly more hearty interest in goings-on around him. I bring him in the newspapers and he looks at the front pages and exclaims, then puts them down. He does not turn on his television. The vicar writes to ask if we may bring some classical music into his life: "It occurs to me that Noel might enjoy some music. There is nothing wrong with his hearing or his eyesight. I don't know how practical this is but I know how much music means to him. Music for those who appreciate it can be a real solace in this situation."

If I think of my father it is of him discreetly conducting index and middle fingers, lightly touching his knee with precision. He is proud of his son, my brother, who was a chorister at Canterbury Cathedral. On my dad's birthday, Christmas Eve, the last time he was well enough to leave the care home, we listened to the start of King's College Carols in the car park in the fading afternoon light. My father bowed his head and tapped to the first lines of "Once in Royal David City". My mother gave him a sharp, solicitous glance, which she had started to do more often. In the mornings, she sometimes asked the nurses if her husband was still alive.

I had found among my father's neat notes in his folder in his study, a paragraph headed "Funeral". He requested that his niece, my cousin, an opera singer, perform Mozart's "Laudate Dominum". And the hymn he asked for was "Immortal Invisible".

The lyrics are about constancy, diligence, justice, solidity, modesty. Hedgehogs rather than foxes. My father is the son of a Methodist chaplain, and I imagined the sound resonating from the Cornish chapels:

… Unresting, unhasting and silent as light,
Nor wanting, nor wasting, thou rulest in might;
Thy justice like mountains high
Soaring above
The clouds which are fountains
Of goodness and love.

To all life thou givest – to both
great and small;
In all life thou livest, the true
Life of all;

We blossom and flourish as
Leaves on the tree,
And wither and perish – but
Nought changes thee.

He wished for cremation. I think he was too modest to want a plot and headstone and liked the idea of being scattered across blessed land or sea, returning to the earth. It is where faith and environmental science seem to agree. We are just atoms, but so are stars.

When I think of him in his final weeks, I would describe his state as attentive and appreciative. Even when he could experience so little of the natural world from his sterile room, he loved it more than ever.

3

WINTER: IN SICKNESS AND IN HEALTH

On a clear, backlit late-January morning, I head to King's Lynn hedgehog hospital to find news of Peggy. The arable fields have a crust of frost and sparkle like crystals. Partridges waddle and peck at the seeds. Winter sunshine bathes the bare spikes of hawthorn hedges. The land is in hibernation, still and patient, but the first shoots are starting to appear. As the earth warms up, patterns of winter and spring are disturbed: how will it affect this prehistorically seasonal mammal, the hedgehog?

Off the main Lynn road, leaving the convey of lorries always on this route at this time of day, I turn into a slip road and then a farm lane, and there, on the corner of a junction, is a white cottage with a new wooden outbuilding next to it. Too large for a shed, too narrow for a studio, it is what Emma calls ICU.

Emma's husband, Mark, a part-time fireman, plumber, electrician, cabinet maker and personal trainer and a full-time devotee of his wife, built the hospital. When my husband brought Peggy here, it was to Emma and Mark's front room. They share their home willingly and Emma often sits in the front room with the hedgehogs as a form of meditation.

She says that the sound of their scratching and snuffling makes her feel calm. "I feel different." When her mother, who was a nurse, died, the hedgehogs had a healing effect on Emma. Their sounds, their curious kindly faces and their Nato armour somehow soothed her.

It is not that they are pets. Despite the medical care that she lavishes on them, picking out vaginal maggots, staring into her microscope to examine their faeces (much of her day is spent looking at faeces), they will never know her as she knows them. They are wild creatures.

In fact, truth be told, they are wild creatures, likely to be carrying ringworm, lungworm, fleas, flies and salmonella. They can transmit these diseases to humans. And yet, to Emma they are magical.

There are boxes across one side of the pristine room and equipment on the other. The boxes, which are clear plastic and lined with shredded newspaper, have names on the outside. Buster, Swift, Titch, Myrtle, Snort, Hercules, Stardust, Swift, Buddy, Loki, Tia Maria: each with a heart next to it. I can hear the soft sound of rustling, snuffling and crunching on biscuits. Emma, who is in her forties and has pink red hair and unhurried, open features, smiles serenely: "The crunching on biscuits is my favourite sound in the world."

Emma is a veterinary nurse who is now vocational about saving hedgehogs. That, she says, is what her mother's death taught her. "I always wanted to learn and better myself and this ignited a purpose in life for me." Her vet surgery has embraced a hedgehog specialism and she describes Dr Nelson as a "hedgehog guru". I make a note to speak to Dr Nelson.

There are delicate operations, including amputations and flushing abscesses. I think: all this for a hedgehog? As if Emma has read my mind, she says that hedgehogs need to be saved because they are in danger of extinction.

On cue, her enviably loving husband Mark appears in the doorway. He says how proud he is of his wife and what she has achieved. He says she has been transformed by hedgehogs.

In between building hospitals, putting out fires and being the only available plumber and electrician in Norfolk so far as I am concerned, he makes tea for the volunteers who turn up to have their hedgehogs' faeces inspected by Emma. I tell Mark he is a marvel. He looks embarrassed and says he only came in to ask if I would mind moving my car so that their daughter – a trainee veterinary nurse – can get out.

Anyway, I ask brightly, how is Peggy getting on? Emma looks down: she says that hedgehogs are usually in a bad way by the time they reach her. If they are out in the day that is usually a bad sign, and worse if they seem wobbly or curled up in the sun. "Maggots will go for every orifice," she says grimly. It is a race against time to get the eggs out before they hatch. The year 2020 was particularly bad for hogs: it was warm and wet and the flies stayed around longer. Then there are ticks.

Country people such as Marc Hamer, author of the wonderful *How to Catch a Mole*, see disease as part of the hedgehog universe.

His poem runs:

A hedgehog,
Its face poxed, with shiny blue-black bodies
Of vile and gorging ticks passed by
I wanted to feel their bodies crush
Like blueberries under my thumb
And the hog's living blood squish out
as the parasites died.

Still they have as much right to life
As the hedgehog and as me
Which is, after all, just chance
To live, or not to live, or die
I let the hedgehog and its crop of ticks go by…

"I used to hate ticks, but I have more respect for them now," says Emma, thoughtfully. The flystrikes get to her more. "It is horrendous," she says. "Especially for the hoglets when they are so *tired* and innocent."

She tears off some paper towel and takes off her spectacles to wipe her eyes. "Sorry, I get emotional."

But it is humans who really frustrate her. The ones who find hedgehogs in peril and wait until the morning to see how they are: 95 per cent of losses are late arrivals.. The ones who give the hogs milk and bread when they are *lactose intolerant* and would do much better with kitten biscuits. The ignorant if well-intentioned ones who put the hedgehogs they find in their conservatories or kitchens, not realising that waking them up like sleeping beauties is dangerous.

Coming out of hibernation is "exhausting" and they burn through calories.

Just *observe*. Is the hog carrying anything in its mouth that might suggest that it is a mother building a nest?

I prick up. There is a school of fancy about what hedgehogs carry, which began with Pliny's *Historia Naturalis*. He wrote: "Hedgehogs prepare food for the winter. They fix fallen apples on their spines by rolling on them and, with an extra one in their mouth, carry them to hollow trees."

Charles Darwin wrote in 1867 that he understood hedgehogs had been seen in the Spanish mountains "trotting along with at least a dozen of these strawberries sticking in their spines... carrying the fruit to their holes to eat in peace".

Emma would also roll her eyes at Aristotle's claim that hedgehogs mate upright on their hind legs.

It is Emma's job, with the help of social media, which, whatever its flaws, is superb at spreading the word on hedgehogs, to follow the science. The route to knowledge is the faeces.

She says with satisfaction: "I have pictures on my phone of hedgehog poo instead of my children."

I chuckle along with the two women volunteers who have joined us in the laboratory. I realise that I am peak demographic for hedgehog watchers (empty nesters, with a bit of time on our hands, wanting to feel needed, looking for something bigger, and, conversely, smaller than ourselves), and that we all watch Emma and her microscope with the same anxious hope for approval.

I wonder which foster parent is looking after Peggy. Emma looks down again.

"Your husband is Kim, isn't he? I am afraid Peggy didn't make it. The maggots were too far into her ears and genitals. We flushed all we could."

As I drove back along the loop to the A17, the sun had turned the ice on the branches to milky drops; the brown featureless canvas of Norfolk at this time of year was stirring into life. Nature was full of hope. But we had lost Peggy. I thought of ways to tell my husband. I am a wife but also a journalist, so breaking news, even bad news, is always slightly thrilling.

And he is a little suspicious that I have followed up

what was really his story. I arranged my features and said, both with sorrowful kindness and relish: "Peggy has passed."

He started, "That's not true, you wicked woman."

I nodded, eyes flashing. "It's true."

It was just a hedgehog. But love is a relationship between dying things. I thought of my dad lying in his nursing home bed looking a little like Francis of Assisi. Skin and bone. And of the tenderness of the young care staff, changing him, propping up his head, giving him protein drinks through a straw. He had given up reading *The Times*, and when I gave him a book that I knew he would love, Simon Jenkins' guide to British cathedrals, he said apologetically: "It is so heavy."

In the first days at the nursing home, he had emailed me that he thought a week would be enough to get himself back in shape; it slipped to a fortnight, then a month, and then we spoke of the spring. He just needed to get his weight back up. We talked of the racket of the rooks making their nests in the trees and the sweet sound of his favourite blackcap singing outside his window. He would be part of the natural world again.

What we could not tell was how much fight he had left in him. In the months of November and December, his large blue eyes, increasingly hollow, would fill with fearful tears. I asked him what was wrong and he said it was just the realisation that this was the end. He was confronting mortality. And his comfort of faith had

The Hedgehog Diaries

deserted him, at this of all times.

I mentioned this to the vicar and he said that doubt was not the enemy. It was natural. And the virtue that counted far beyond certainty was perseverance. I needed my father to persevere. Later, I discovered that it was science as much as soul behind the tears. Heart failure hits the area of your brain that affects the emotions.

The Winter Solstice came and we braced ourselves for loss. I sat by my father's bedside remembering the words of the Archbishop of Canterbury to me on the essence of ministry: "It is holding the hands of the dying."

Also at his bedside, and with the greatest claim on him, was my mother. The dynamic of their relationship had changed; before his collapse, he was the carer, now she worried if his hands and feet were cold – circulation drying up. My mother had never much liked Norfolk, but she settled into the room next to my father like a sentry guard. The two of them approaching the end of life's long journey and realising that a marriage is founded on memory. Perhaps the soul could also be described as memory. The years vanished and they were in love again. Love is a relationship between dying things.

It turned out to be shocking that an old man was coming to the end of his life. I explained this to Giles Fraser, the priest and rebel, who is a regular on *Thought for the Day*. Why was I so upset? He replied that bereavement could not be categorised by age.

My mother also put it neatly: "You just don't expect this to happen at our time of life." I nodded sympathetically and then we both began laughing. What else do you expect to happen?

But my father was the interesting one. Out of time, greatly loved and now barely living, he was not prepared to throw in the towel. His faith may have wavered but not his belief in the astonishing and infinite preciousness of life. You do not leave it a moment before you have to. I realised that this was a mark of his two chief characteristics: appreciation and humility.

The bed became the focus of existence. He began to forget there had been other rooms; that moving from bedroom to kitchen, to his green tweed armchair with the sight of blue tits washing in the bird bath, had signalled rhythms of the day.

The familiar becomes unimaginable: walking to post a letter. I remind him how, only three months ago, I had taken him to look for pink-footed geese at Holkham on the north coast. Now, he can only haul himself a few yards to the bathroom, and if he does so, emergency alarms go off and nurses run in, in case he falls.

What he needed to do was conserve his energy: the hedgehog knows all about this with its bed of leaves, filled with insects. It turns out that our compost heap of garden leaves writhing with worms is just grand. Our garden is one great leaf drop. It was created around beech trees and beech hedges. I knew it suited Billy, our grandson, to kick the leaves and to help rake them until he grew bored but I had not thought of the garden as a hedgehog housing development.

The hedgehog curls up and its heart rate slows. Its body temperature drops from 34°C to 2°C and it hardly breathes at all. It is cold to the touch.

I know what to look out for with my dad. His pulse must not beat too fast, his blood pressure must not sink too low. His tired old heart can just about keep going on a cocktail of drugs but exertion will kill him. This is his equilibrium; just about living.

I tell him that he has chosen the right season in which to hibernate. He loses track of the days and of weather. I tell him each time I visit that it is cold, or windy or sunny, but in the nursing home room the temperature is constant.

The hedgehog can live on its fat through the season but my dad cannot. My sister and I feed him bananas; my son passes gym drinks through the window (visitors are limited). My grandson waves cheerily from outside, putting his lips steamily to the glass: "What you doing in there?"

Christmas passes and the snowdrops arrive in January. Dusk falls slightly later. Despite some near misses with late-night visits to Norwich hospital, my father hangs on. If we could just reach the spring.

In her book *The Hedgehog Handbook*, Susan Coulthard signals that February is the turning point: "In the hibernaculum, the hedgehog's enforced isolation is nearly at an end. In just a few weeks she'll wake from her slumber hungry and much thinner, but ready to start the year's cycle all over again."

Some survive, some do not. At the end of January, Emma posted that three hedgehogs had been taken to see Dr Nelson. Primrose and Clivette got the all-clear. Trevor, the Santa hog, could not keep up.

"Trevor, aka Santa hog, a mature gentleman, arrived on Christmas Eve very underweight and full of parasites and ringworm. He started to thrive and was doing really well until just recently a lump started to grow on one of his limbs and despite eating he was losing weight daily. On investigation yesterday it was confirmed that Trevor had cancer. I really hope Trevor is running free over rainbow bridge chasing all the bugs with no pain or discomfort. Thank you to Dr Nelson @Millhouse Veterinary Hospital."

And then, having told Kim about the "passing of Peggy", I receive a message from Emma:

"Peggy is your Peggy!!! My apologies. I've just looked back at her admit form. Your husband brought her in on the 17.10. She had flystrike in her genitals."

Peggy is alive and will be coming home in the spring. If all is well, she will be released back into our garden.

A few miles on from the Queen Elizabeth Hospital where my father was taken in the late autumn of 2021, is the Mill House Veterinary Clinic and Hospital. Inside the red brick building, next to a university campus, are defibrillators and gleaming equipment for X-rays and ultrasound. It is busy because of the sharp rise in pet ownership during the pandemic but the staff are not overwhelmed or exhausted in the way those at the Queen Elizabeth Hospital became.

This is the place where Emma works as a veterinary nurse and where her friend Helen Nelson is a doctor. Hedgehogs have a special place here. Helen was brought up in Lynn, with hedgehogs in the garden, and she went on to volunteer in the wildlife centre before studying veterinary science. Aged 39, she has observed hedgehogs most of her life. What strikes her fundamentally about them is their will to survive.

They have got through evolution and they have managed to outlive roads, dogs, strimmers and pesticides, although their numbers are dwindling and they may not survive the future.

The other characteristic loved by Helen is their equilibrium. They are not highly strung and fearful in the manner of deer. They are not aggressive, in the way of badgers who, beautiful as they are, can use jaw, teeth and claws to lethal effect – especially on hedgehogs.

Hedgehogs are not afraid of humans, although neither do they seek their company. They are self-contained. They will not resist or run or fight. The will simply curl up. Helen talks about the pleasure of handling them compared to some other wild creatures. It is easy to find the softness and the suppleness.

She does not think of them as pets but she recognises individual characteristics. Some are more outgoing, some shyer. Males are bigger and smellier, which is of course generally the case. None is social, however, and they remain mysterious. For a start they are nocturnal, and walk for miles while humans sleep. They can co-exist with humans, with some consideration on our part. But they are not tamed by humans. The comparison she makes is with the robin, who can stay close to humans but is not of their world. It is only that humans in the garden may lead them to worms.

The injuries treated by Dr Nelson speak to the perils faced by hedgehogs. If they break a leg in a fall, it may require amputation. They can be injured by dogs, and can be stitched so long as facial injuries are not too severe. Since their eyesight is poor, they need to be able to smell and hear. The worst injuries come from badgers or strimmers.

Strimmers can slice through the middle of their spines, dividing them in half. The injuries caused by badgers are chilling. They flip them over, tear open their stomachs and pull out their intestines.

In the same way as Emma, Helen likes to sit by the hedgehog cases in clinics and listen. The curious snuffling sound provides the same emotional balm as listening to horses munching hay in a stable.

She just hopes that the individual will to live will enable the survival of the species. "However ill they are, they will always try to eat. There is such a determination to survive whatever stage they are at. It would be terrible to think that they might become extinct."

I too am thinking about survival but also bracing myself for hopelessness. I ask the same questions of my father

– how is he eating? How is he sleeping? – and he answers positively. Why then does he continue to lose weight? My mother asks the question we dare not answer: "Why isn't he getting better?"

It was the founder of the hospice movement, Cicely Saunders, who when asked by a patient of whom she was fond whether he was dying, dared to reply: "Yes."

Even when my father could no longer stand unaided, he did not talk of dying. I don't think he was denying it but he never gave up hope. It was a supreme modesty. It was out of his hands and he only wanted to make the most of all remaining moments.

"What are the plans?" he would ask. I would tell him that I was going to bring him a glass of his favourite local South Pickenham sparkling wine and then there would be Six Nations rugby on the television.

"Oh good," he would say, eyes shining. He slept through the rugby. "I am so idle these days," he said.

Cicely Saunders spent her life making death part of medicine but she was not in favour of assisted dying, believing that the right to die might become a duty to die. Hers, and my father's way, was acceptance.

Cicely Saunders used a quote by one of her patients – "all of me is wrong" – to demonstrate how palliative medicine aims to care for the dying holistically.

Dying is not simply a medical issue, it is public, social, spiritual. The Rev Kit Chalcraft was right: if it is too late for poetry, there can still be music. He and my father listened to the exuberant Beethoven Fourth

Symphony. And Kit and I slipped our hands into my father's: the simplest final act, holding the hand of the dying.

4

MRS TIGGY-WINKLE AND THE POETRY OF HEDGEHOGS

On February 24, the day that Russia invaded Ukraine, visitors poured into the Victoria and Albert Museum to see an exhibition about Beatrix Potter and the natural world. There is no need to underline the differences between the world of President Putin's mad fantasies of Russian domination and that of *The Tale of Little Pig Robinson*, whose characters led "prosperous uneventful lives".

The comic writer Craig Brown suggested in the *Daily*

Mail suitable subjects to take our mind off the apocalyptic war. His first suggested title was "How the hedgehog safely crossed the road".

Beatrix Potter's father, Rupert Potter, was a Northern Unitarian, who, according to the family biography *Over the Hills and Far Away* by Matthew Dennison, had "a terror of any disturbance or violence" and preferred quiet provincial towns to the fashionable metropolis.

Many of the visitors at the V and A the day that I went to the exhibition had Yorkshire or Cumbrian accents but there were foreign tourists too. The day that the world order collapsed and tyranny broke free, there was a yearning to study the habits of dormice.

Cities lost their lustre during the pandemic, but Beatrix Potter made her mind up about that more than 150 years ago. She said that London was her "unloved home" and her joy was the North and nature. She observed nature as Gilbert White had done before her, and her drawings at the V and A drew murmurs of pleasure as glasses steamed up with the hot breath under the face masks. The hedgehog pictures have a sophisticated range of colour and accurately drawn snouts. They are both anatomical and full of character. Beatrix Potter kept a specimen cabinet for fossils, eggs and butterflies. She visited the Natural History Museum to make copies of geological specimens. She was looked down on by the academic scientists of the day, at Kew and Cambridge, but encouraged by our old friend the country parson amateur naturalist. In this case, it was Hardwicke

Rawnsley, rector of Wray-on-Windermere and founder of the Lake District Defence Society.

Potter had a special relationship with British wild life, writing: "I seem to be able to tame any sort of animal." This included hedgehogs. It was a pet female hedgehog who was the inspiration for Mrs Tiggy-Winkle. "She was not a bit prickly with me, she used to lay her prickles flat to be stroked."

Potter took advice from the pre-Raphaelite painter John Everett Millais, who wrote, advising her to "take the world as we find it". This, surely, is hedgehog wisdom.

When Potter lost the love of her life, Norman Warne, the son of her publisher, who then took charge of her books, to lymphatic leukaemia, it was nature that was her balm. She describes it almost in the language of Resurrection: "I remember thinking the evening was as still as death – and as beautiful… As I was looking at it, there came out through the mist over the sea just for a few seconds – a gleam of golden sunshine – 'In the evening there shall be Light.'"

She joined the Society for the Preservation of Ancient Buildings, founded by William Morris, and later married a vicar's son, William Heelis. The *Westmoreland Gazette* described the wedding as "the quietest of quiet manners". The couple led a prosperous, uneventful life farming 4000 acres and two flocks of Herdwick sheep.

In order to understand Mrs Tiggy-Winkle, you have to spend time in the Lake District. The first enchantment is the air: in the autumn, it's icy clean and tinged with woodsmoke; in the spring, sweet-smelling snowdrops are the prelude for the floral opera to come: carpets of bluebells, primroses and wild daffodils.

The second enchantment is the light: which lingers for at least an hour or two longer than anywhere south. You can scramble up the fells for further time travel, chasing the sun upwards, before you give out on a craggy rock, terrifically exhausted. The sun creeps down again – one last flash of burning red splendour before it finally disappears. No wonder Beatrix Potter loved it here so dearly. This is a landscape of children's fantasy. Mountains, fells, wild ferns, exotic mushrooms, hilltop meadows, bubbling streams, waterfalls, tarns and lakes. It is the perfect location for the equally fantastical hedgehog.

Beatrix Potter's lost love Norman Warne was originally against the book proposal for Mrs Tiggy-Winkle. He cautioned that "dirty hedgehogs wouldn't appeal to children — probably because they're not fluffy". This seems rather strange to us now. It's hard to imagine the hedgehog as our disease-ridden enemy. Yet, before Tiggy, it seems that "hedgehog" was firmly used as a pejorative. In Shakespeare's *Richard the Third*, Lady Anne assails Gloucester with the word prior to his coronation; and the fairies banish the creature along with snakes, newts and worms in *A Midsummer's Night Dream*.

Beatrix Potter, with her rare animal sense and creaturely intuition, had no time for such binaries. She welcomed bats, frogs, snakes, lizards and hedgehogs into her school room at home. She observed and drew her collection compulsively, and, in true Victorian style, would boil down her pets when they died, so she could draw the skeletons (yes – even bunnies).

Her childhood was an odd mix of freedom and restraint. She grew up in Kensington, where her Unitarian parents sat awkwardly among the traditional upper classes. As non-conformists, the family were outcast from smart society, and their social insecurity meant Beatrix and her younger brother Bertie had few friends their own age. Her mother, Helen, was a difficult, controlling woman whom Beatrix came to denote as "the enemy" in her diary.

The young Potter sought companionship and imaginative escape through the lives and characters of her pets. Her private zoo, as you might imagine, came with a good deal of domestic adventure. One journal entry starts, 'Sally the snake and four black newts escaped overnight. Caught one black newt in school room and another in larder, but nothing seen of poor Sally.' Her own bid for freedom would have to wait until she was in her late thirties, when she signed the contact for *Peter Rabbit*, and earned her financial independence.

She made her first sketches of Mrs Tiggy-Winkle in the summer of 1904, when she was in the Lakes for a holiday. The charming hamlet of Little Town near Keswick, along with the Newlands valley and mountain of Skiddaw, provided the backdrop. The small door to Mrs Tiggy's cottage was sketched from an entrance to an abandoned mine shaft. It's this mix of naturalist observation and imaginative fantasy that's so delightful about Potter's illustrations. It's often noted that all her animals are anatomically correct – rare in children's books these days – because she drew from real life. And so, it would be her pet hedgehog, the real Mrs Tiggy, who modelled for the preliminary illustrations (she moved on to a doll to capture the full bonneted figure). Potter was affectionate, if not exactly sentimental, towards her somewhat impertinent subject. In a letter to Norman, she wrote:

> So long as she can go to sleep on my knee she is delighted, but if she is propped up on end for half an hour, she first begins to yawn pathetically, and then she does bite! Nevertheless, she is a dear person; just like a very fat rather stupid little dog.

It's not a particularly flattering portrait, but it's an improvement on "dirty". Mrs Tiggy-Winkle is depicted as fantastically round, with her hands clasped endearingly under her fat, fuzzy cheeks and wearing a quaint little pinafore. With this comical illustration, Potter has brought the hedgehog into a realm of dearness.

Perhaps all it took was propping up the hedgehog on its hind legs. Cuteness is a rather simplistic aesthetic – the smaller and rounder the better. On Instagram, there are plenty of pictures of hedgehogs lying flat on their backs and receiving a tickling. I see a hedgehog in Tokyo called Darcy has over 300,000 followers and is always looking like an overturned beetle. In one photo, she wears a chef's hat and clutches a tiny pan, in the next she is on a dinner plate, between a knife and fork. It's not quite clear whether we're supposed to squidge her or eat her.

This uneasy relationship between hedgehog and human is not missed by Potter. For all the comforting cuteness and domesticity of Mrs Tiggy-Winkle, this is a character with a few prickles. Potter's secondary source of inspiration was Kitty Macdonald, a Scottish washerwoman whom the family employed over the summers at their country house in Perthshire. Mrs Tiggy-Winkle is more of a matronly figure than a motherly one, and the child protagonist Lucie is set apart not only by species, but also by Victorian class.

The story follows Lucie as she searches for her lost items of clothing, "three handkins and a pinny". She asks Tabby Kitten and Sally Henny-Penny, who are both indifferent to her predicament. The hen is not bound by the laws of humans and Victorian England. She tells Lucie, with a casual hen-like cluck, "I go barefoot, barefoot, barefoot". The robin gives Lucie a "sideways" look and flies far, far away. Lucie continues in her quest, scrambling up the valley until she reaches a bubbling spring and sees "the foot-marks of a very small person". There, cut into the rock, is a small door, the perfect height for a child. Mrs Tiggy-Winkle is not exactly thrilled about her surprise guest. She calls out in "a little frightened voice", stares "anxiously" and addresses the child with a formal "bob-curtsey". It seems Lucie has traversed both magical and domestic boundaries.

Tiggy soon accommodates Lucie, however, showing the little girl her latest handwork. It seems that poor Tiggy is run off her feet, managing the laundry for all the animals in the valley. There's Robin's waistcoat, Wren's tablecloth, Henny's stockings, Rabbit's handkersniff, Kitten's mittens, Titmouse's shirtfronts, woolly coats for the lambs, Squirrel Nutkin's tailcoat, Peter Rabbit's jacket, and – of course – Lucie's missing handkins and pinny.

It's not quite companionship. There is naturally some distance between an obliging servant and a curious child. Lucie notes Tiggy's hands, "very very brown, and very very wrinkly from all the soap suds" and her prickles (or hair-pins) sticking out from her gown and cap, so that "Lucie didn't like to sit too near to her".

Prickles – the defining characteristic of the hedgehog – together with its magical ability to roll into a ball make for an animal full of contradiction. Thorny and tender, wild and tame, powerful and defenceless. In some sense, Norman was right, the hedgehog is not simply a children's toy.

It's this shifting ambiguity that has captured the imagination of poets and philosophers. In fact, it was Jacques Derrida who made the jump to see the hedgehog as a metaphor for poetry itself. He was commissioned by an Italian poetry journal to write a response to the question: "*Che cos'è la poesia?*" or "What is poetry?" His answer: *le hérisson*. He takes his cue from an earlier philosopher, Friedreich von Schlegel, who wrote that a poem "must be totally detached from the surrounding world and closed in on itself like a hedgehog". Derrida takes this idea further.

We're told to imagine a hedgehog lying rolled up, for self-defence, in the middle of the road. Its defence, Derrida tells us, is "in the same stroke" what exposes the hedgehog to death from an oncoming car. This, he argues, is like a poem. A poem protects itself by refusing to be totally understood, but in doing so it faces being ignored and forgotten. The poem, like the hedgehog, is a vulnerable thing – it asks us as readers to "learn me by heart, copy me down, guard and keep me, look out for me". With proper care, the hedgehog – or the poem – lays down its spikes and opens up to us. The phrase "learn by heart", he points out, has an equivalent in almost every language. Poems, like hedgehogs, pull on our emotional heartstrings, they bring out something protective and maternal in us.

This might strike you as a little sentimental for a philosopher who's more commonly associated with the prickly ideas of atheism and deconstruction. In fact, Derrida was a passionate friend of animals and made moving arguments for what might be called animal rights – although this phrase, he says, is part of the problem. Ever attuned to language, Derrida sees the word "animal" as an oppressive tool that reinforces human dominance.

The animal, what a word! It is an appellation that

men have instituted, a name they have given themselves the right and the authority to give to the living other... in spite of the infinite space that separates the lizard from the dog, the protozoon from the dolphin, the shark from the lamb, the parrot from the chimpanzee, the camel from the eagle, the squirrel from the tiger, the elephant from the cat, the ant from the silkworm, or the hedgehog from the echidna. Interrupt my nomenclature and call Noah to help ensure that no one gets left on the ark.

Derrida is at odds with Western philosophy, which either ignores the lives of animals outright or denies that they are conscious beings. Heidegger wrote that animals are "poor in world" while humans are "world forming". This superiority, Derrida argues, originates in Christian ideology. In Genesis, God states that humankind shall have "dominion over the fish of the sea, and over the birds of the air, and over the cattle, and over all the wild animals of the earth, and over every creeping thing that creeps upon the earth". Today's climate consciousness doesn't sit well with this. Our relationship with animals has become heavily degraded by the demands of mass production – something Derrida was aware of back in the 60s. He saw the "conditions that previous generations would have judged monstrous": the battery farms and steady annihilation of natural habitats. Indeed, like Derrida, contemporary writers have made a direct correlation between climate disaster and Western, humanist ideology. In *Straw Dogs*, John Gray blames humanism, and the belief that we have "dominion" over living creatures, for much of the destruction of the natural world.

In Hindu culture, the relationship with animals is very different. They are believed to have souls, just like humans, and certain doctrines mandate vegetarianism. Contemporary science is revealing that this belief may well be correct, in a radical reassessment of previously held assumptions. In 2012, a prominent group of scientists published *The Cambridge Declaration on Consciousness*, which declared that a significant number of animals, including invertebrates like the octopus, are conscious beings. Our culture is catching up with this: in lockdown, the documentary *My Octopus Teacher*, which explored the relationship between a diver and an octopus, sent shockwaves into the world – and I'll certainly be thinking twice before digging into a polpo sandwich at the Italian deli. Similarly, the new documentary *Cow* by Andrea Arnold is a close portrait of the life and death of a dairy cow. In the opening sequence, the cow is separated from her calf and becomes withdrawn and unable to eat. I still can't quite bring myself to watch it.

To return to Derrida, the question of animals, he says, is a simple one. All we need ask is "do they suffer?" and, if the answer is yes, then we must ask the second, more difficult question: "why do we make them do so?" In a knock-out discursive finale, he says this:

Let me simply say a word about this "pathos". If these images are "pathetic", if they evoke sympathy, it is also because they "pathetically" open the immense question of pathos and the pathological, precisely, that is, of suffering, pity and compassion.

How do you like that for sentimental? Our failure to protect hedgehogs is an existential failure, a symbol – and symptom – of our alienation from the living world (interestingly, the word animal comes from the Latin *anima*, meaning "living"). No one knew this better, of course, than Samuel Beckett, whose morbid account of a failed hedgehog rescue in his play *Company* was based on his own childhood misstep.

He takes pity on a hedgehog out in the cold, bringing it inside and putting it "in an old hatbox" in a disused hutch, wedged open so the hedgehog can go at will. Later, he is "faintly glowing" at the thought of his "good deed" and believes the hedgehog was fortunate to have crossed paths with him. What follows is one of the most sinister passages I think I've come across – it may need a trigger warning for hedgehog lovers.

Now the next morning not only was the glow spent but a great uneasiness had taken its place. A suspicion that all was perhaps not as it should be. That rather than do as you did you had perhaps better let good alone and the hedgehog pursue its way. Days if not weeks passed before you could bring yourself to return to the hutch. You have never forgotten what you found then. You are on your back in the dark and have never forgotten what you found then. The mush. The stench.

The poor child faces the stinging reality of his clumsy human intervention. The same could be said for Ted Hughes and his own failed "rescue", when he finds his hedgehog "sobbing like a little child"... "his nose pressed in a pool of tears, and his face all wet, and snivelling and snuffling his heart out".

Hedgehogs are weary travellers of the domestic human boundary, ever being picked up, displaced and mishandled. It's not easy owning up to our many abuses, whether we mean to commit them or not. Poet Paul Muldoon explores this in his poem, "Hedgehog", in which the creature takes on a devastating cynicism.

Here, the hedgehog will not open itself up to us, no matter how much we want to love it.

...The hedgehog
Shares its secret with no one.
We say, Hedgehog, come out
Of yourself and we will love you.

We mean no harm. We want
Only to listen to what
You have to say. We want
Your answers to our questions.

The hedgehog gives nothing
Away, keeping itself to itself.
We wonder what a hedgehog
Has to hide, why it so distrusts.

We forget the god
Under this crown of thorns.
We forget that never again
Will a god trust in the world.

There is a twist at the end of Mrs Tiggy-Winkle. When the child, Lucie, turns to say goodbye, she finds that Mrs Tiggy-Winkle has disappeared. She has not waited "either for thanks or for the washing bill". Then, suddenly, Lucie catches sight of her, "running running up the hill". But it is not Mrs Tiggy-Winkle at all – for where are her white frilled cap, her gown and her petticoat? Why, Mrs Tiggy-Winkle is nothing but a hedgehog. And, as a hedgehog should be – safe to roam and just out of grasp.

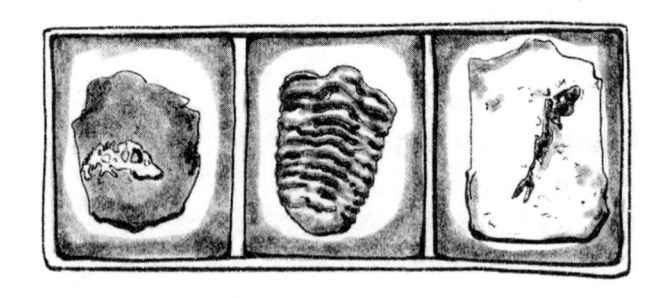

5

PREHISTORIC HEDGEHOGS AND DUSKING

I am thinking again of Rory Stewart's speech about hedgehogs, and how the hedgehog, and its ancestor, "narrowly missed being crushed under the foot of Tyrannosaurus Rex". It is the sheer age of the species that is humbling. One foot in front of the other for millions of years.

At the Natural History Museum, there is a fossil of a hedgehog skeleton from the Middle Eocene period, between 56 and 33 million years ago. It is on the run with hind legs at full stretch beneath a heavy pelvis and... a tail.

The curator of fossil mammals, Dr Spyridoula Pappa, is showing me her treasure after a little tour of filing cabinets of jawbones from Darwin's Beagle Voyage. Roula, as she calls herself, is dressed like a beauteous slender lizard chanteuse in a long green dress with a black T-shirt, and contemporary earrings. Above her black face mask, she has vivid dark eyes and shaped eyebrows, and glossy hair.

Her eyes cloud slightly at my response. I say that the hedgehog looks rather like a rat. She says sternly: "The hedgehog is not a rodent."

I am forgiven, and shown further trays of tiny flints. Looking to have narrowly missed being crushed by a dinosaur is a tiny two-inch hedgehog, the size of a shrew, whose remains, found in British Columbia, are 52 million years old.

Roula next lovingly holds up, in plastic gloves, a portion of a skull found in France – it is a spiny, caramel-and-toffee-coloured fossil.

There is mention, though no remains here, of a prehistoric giant hedgehog, thought to have lived in Italy in the Late Miocene. I think of the barrow of trees on a hill near Avebury in Wiltshire known locally as the "three hedgehogs in a line".

I think, too, of West Runton, near Cromer in north Norfolk, with its forest bed of peat at the bottom of the cliff, packed with fossils. It is of a later period but rich in small mammals and bird bones. It was the Quaternary period, which started 2.6 millions years ago, that eventually produced another predator, humans, to crush the hedgehog.

Roula points through the microscope to another hedgehog specimen with the faintest mark of a cut across it. Seemingly, the specimen predates the use of fire. So we are right at the start of our human ancestry.

Hedgehogs have been eaten until quite recently and remain a traditional dish for Romanies and roadkill chefs. There is an elaborate recipe quoted in *A Prickly Affair*, a seminal work by Hugh Warwick, the aforementioned David Attenborough of hedgehogs, whom we will hear more from later. The recipe comes from "An Account of the Moorish Way of Dressing Their Meat" by Jezreel Jones, which was published in Royal Society's *Philosophical Transactions* in 1699.

> The Hedgehog is a Princely Dish amongst them, and before they kill him, rub his Back against the Ground, by holding its Feet betwixt two, as Men do a Saw that Saws stones, till it had done squeaking; then they cut its Throat and with a Knife cut off all its Spines and singe it. They take out its Guts, stuff the Body with some Rice, sweet Herbs, Garavancas, Spice and Onions; they put some Butter and Garavancas into the Water they stew it in and let it stew in a little Pot close stopped till it is enough and it proves an excellent Dish.

The cut marks found on fossil hedgehogs (*Erina-*

ceous broomei) in Olduvai Gorge in Tanzania yielded valuable behavioural information about our species and theirs. A piece was published in the *Journal of Human Evolution* in 1999 entitled "Cut marks on small mammals at Olduvai Gorge Bed-1", explaining that academics had recorded that "cut marks on the hedgehog mandibles have an oblique arrangement and characteristic micromorphology which distinguishes them from trampling marks".

The notes go on to say that this relates to "skinning activities" rather than "de-fleshing". I shudder thinking of what badgers do. Humans were at least a little more delicate in their methods of killing hedgehogs.

There are other fossils in Roula's office, displayed like jewels in their trays. From Switzerland, a tiny fragment of a recognisably long snout. From Africa, a formation of bones.

With us is Stephanie Holt, Biodiversity Training Manager at the Natural History Museum. Her special subject is bats, but hedgehogs come a close second. She breathes over the trays of fossils: "Fossils allow you to time-travel, hedgehogs past, present and future."

Stephanie has a russet glow, with her pre-Raphaelite hair, outdoor skin and luminous pleasure in her vocation of conservation.

"The thing about hedgehogs is that they are still a bit of a mystery to us," she says, sitting down on a green sofa beneath a map of wild spaces and portraits of two great British naturalists, Mary Anning, "the fossil

The Hedgehog Diaries

woman" of Dorset, and Gilbert White, the eighteenth-century country parson and amateur natural historian.

In front of us is a fine specimen of a hedgehog preserved by taxidermy. It is on the move and its legs have some of the length of the early fossil that I rudely mistook for a rodent. Its museum nickname is Linford. I am learning to spot slight distinctions in colouring, and this one has sun-bleached spikes. I think I would recognise him if I saw him again.

Paying attention to detail is what makes an accomplished natural historian. Beatrix Potter kept meticulous records of appearance and behaviour, in the tradition of Gilbert White. Stephanie if a big fan of White, because he defined an English approach of observation rather than lofty pronouncements.

Before Gilbert White, our natural history was handed down as gospel from the Romans. Stephanie exclaims: "We just copied whatever Pliny said!"

I remember the preposterous education of Pliny's *Historia Naturalis*. "Hedgehogs prepare food for the winter. They fix fallen apples on their spines by rolling on them and, with an extra one in their mouth, carry them to hollow trees."

For Stephanie, the first profoundly true description of a hedgehog was made by White in 1770.

Instead of offering scientific examination of a dead specimen, Gilbert White captured what it meant to be a hedgehog. Were we to describe Linford, the Natural History Museum specimen, we might say that it is a long-legged spiky creature designed for running. We would not know that it curled up, or more precisely that it frowned first. Gilbert White preferred to "observe narrowly". He wrote to his friend Thomas Pennant, author of *British Zoology*, as follows:

Gilbert White to Thomas Pennant, Selborne, Feb 22, 1770.

Dear Sir,
Hedge-hogs abound in my garden and fields. The manner in which they eat the roots of the plantain in my grass walks is very curious: with their upper mandible, which is much longer than their lower, they bore under the plant, and so eat the root off upwards, leaving the tuft of leaves untouched. In this respect the are serviceable, as they destroy a very troublesome weed: but they deface the walks in some measure by digging little round holes. It appears, by the dung that they drop upon the turf, that beetles are no inconsiderable part of their food.

In June last I procured a litter of four or five young hedge-hogs, which appeared to be about five or six days old; they, I find, like puppies, are born blind, and could not see when they came to my hands. No doubt their spines are soft and flexible at the time of their birth, or else the poor dam would have but a bad time of it in the critical moment of parturition: but it is plain that they soon harden; for these little pigs had such stiff prickles on their backs and sides as would easily have fetched blood had they not been handled with caution.

Their spines are quite white at this stage; and they have little hanging ears, which I do not remember to be discernible in the old ones. They can, in part, at this age draw their skin down over their faces; but are not able to contract themselves into a ball, as they do, for the sake of defence, when full grown.

The reason, I suppose, is, because the curious muscle that enables the creature to roll itself up in a ball was not then arrived at its full tone and firmness. Hedge-hogs make a deep and warm hibernaculum with leaves and moss, in which they conceal themselves for the winter: but I never could find that they stored in any winter provision, as some quadrupeds certainly do...

Stephanie is transported by the detail of the observation. Nobody had described before a juvenile hedgehog, identified by its white spikes.

"He must have found a hedgehog nest," she says, eyes dancing.

Observation matters because there is still much we do not know about hedgehogs. It is hard to keep an eye on them when they just disappear from sight. Because of my new-found interest in them, I scour hedges or stop when I see something that turns out to be a stone or brush. The roadkill measurement is certainly no longer reliable. For a start, it is behavioural. How many hedgehogs set out across the road? Perhaps hedgehogs have become more road-safety conscious, but that sounds like the Pliny version to me. I am afraid Gilbert White might conclude that there are just far fewer hedgehogs. Certainly in Norfolk, I see many squashed pheasants now the shooting season is over, and rabbits and muntjac and badgers, but no hedgehogs.

It is interesting that we have such a clear image of hedgehogs when it is so rare to see one. We have mostly to thank Beatrix Potter for that, but also school and community projects run by hedgehog volunteers.

Stephanie's specialism, bats, are also under threat, with some species down by 90 per cent. They are a harder sell, never having been drawn by Beatrix Potter, but Stephanie doughtily draws parallels. Like hedgehogs, they are nocturnal, secretive and poor-sighted and they suffer from the same curse of pesticides affecting their prey. Soil is the foundation of life.

What fascinates Stephanie – and now me – about hedgehogs is their evolutionary survival. They tell us about the state of our world.

"Hedgehogs are the great indicator. They are a relatively old species," says Stephanie (for 35 million years or so is relative in the Natural History Museum). "They indicate whether you have a good environment and a well-connected landscape."

We can design landscapes for hedgehogs, of allotments and ponds and scrub. But does it work? I have done all this, and yet I still cannot account for my hedgehog.

This triumph of evolution now has to survive the age of the Anthropocene. And the legislative spur to the state of the badger.

The big test, says Stephanie, will be if and how hedgehogs adapt to climate change. Will their defining habit of hibernation change? Will they stay awake for longer or stop hibernating altogether during warmer, wetter winters? New Zealand is an interesting test case. In North Island, the hedgehogs do not hibernate because there is always something to eat. In South Island, they do hibernate. Is there any physiological damage caused by such a drastic metabolic change?

Their weight, so minutely monitored by Emma and the volunteers in all the other hedgehog hospitals, becomes an issue. Should they or should they not bulk up for winter? Then, if the warmer season lingers, is there time for a second or third brood? And if so, will this produce weaker juveniles? The changing pressures on the species require further study and Stephanie is desperate for a research grant to do it.

Apart from climate, the main threat to the species are predators, which divide more or less evenly between badgers and those road hogs, humans.

I ask indignantly why badgers attack and Stephanie answers pragmatically: "Because they can. There is a lovely chunk of protein moving quite slowly in front of them. The success of badgers in population numbers has an effect on a species that is struggling."

The hedgehog's solitary nature exposes it to badgers, although gathering in groups would probably not make them any less vulnerable.

"There is no advantage in clustering together; better spread yourself around the landscape so you are harder to find," advises Stephanie.

As if to remind me of possible fates, Stephanie shakes out some skeleton leg pieces from a jar. Her point is that the actual leg bones are quite long, but you don't normally see them because hedgehogs hover.

Of the two questions most often asked about hedgehogs we have touched on the unhappy one: their relationship with badgers. I shall return to this in a later chapter. The jollier question is about their mating habits. Rarely seen, never forgotten.

How do hedgehogs mate? It turns out that the female lifts up her skirt. Probably the best piece of work on this is a poem by Terry Pratchett, the one happily *not* played by mistake when the former Archbishop of Canterbury appeared on *Desert Island Discs*:

The Hedgehog Can Never Be Buggered At All

Bestiality sure is a fun thing to do
But I have to say this as a warning to you
With almost all animals you can have a ball
But the hedgehog can never be buggered at all

Chorus: The spines on his back are too sharp for
>
> a man
>
They'll give you a pain in the worst place they can
The result I think you'll find will appal
The hedgehog can never be buggered at all…

So it continues. Mating with hedgehogs is certainly not advised for humans but within the species it is an amazing sight. And sound.

Stephanie clasps her hands at the memory of it: "I have come across mating hedgehogs and, WOW, are they noisy. Last time it was when I was doing a bat survey. I was in the garden and it was getting dark. Suddenly, two hedgehogs started mating behind me. The sounds are hilarious, such a bizarre noise, like a steam train, and quite a vocal range. I think the noise comes from the female."

Some people, such as Lord Goldsmith, who would like the hedgehog to be a national symbol of Britain post-Brexit might want to play down the fact that ours is the European hedgehog, which crossed the land bridge into Britain just as the ice age was coming to an end and sea levels were starting to rise. An ancient creature, which comes to life at dusk.

That's why dusk is Stephanie's favourite time. She describes it as the shift change, the moment when the birds stop singing and "you can feel a point on your cheek where the temperature changes". During this little lull, when all is quiet and the day shift has gone to bed, you might still see the odd goose, but there is a change. You might hear a slight rustling in the hedge, you might get the first bat popping out, just to check the sparrow hawks have returned to their roosts. And then a little bit after that you might start to hear a little snuffling going on. Mrs Tiggy-Winkle.

When the world is put to rights, the rustle from the hedgerow will be followed by a crackling of leaves. This will happen in a garden full of crab apples and pears and damsons, with different habitats, dampness for earthworms, ponds for slugs. And let's hope a garden without the new fashion for drone lawnmowers at night.

We seem to be back to the wisdom of hedgehogs and Isaiah Berlin. What is it, I ask Stephanie, that a hedgehog knows? Stephanie is too true to science to allow hedgehogs an imagined wisdom.

"There is not a lot going on with hedgehogs," she says. "The brain-to-body size is in odd proportion, and compared to other insectivores, pound for pound they have a much smaller brain size than, say, a shrew."

"So they are not very clever after all?" I ask in dismay.

"They are very good at being hedgehogs. Better at being a hedgehog than I am. Maybe not so good at abstract thought."

6

THE RELEASE OF PEGGY

I am at a diplomatic dinner at the Athenaeum Club, in Pall Mall, London, discussing the Ukraine crisis. A former secretary general of Nato talks of the delicate balance between strength and diplomacy and the importance of a united front.

A text pings on my phone. It is about our symbol of Nato. Emma says that Peggy, our sick hedgehog, is ready to be returned to the wild. It has to be tomorrow night. I can fetch her from the hospital in a box. "Have you got a hedgehog house to release her into or a nice big log pile?"

I text back weakly under the table that the following evening is tricky. I am busy with appointments and wonder if we could wait until the weekend. The response is immediate: "Oh no! Let me check temps. Release window ideally tomorrow as gives time to settle for two days."

I cannot argue with ideal conditions for survival. I clear my diary and the following morning drive to Norfolk. Luckily, I remember that our younger son had bought us a fine mossy hog house which we hid by the beech trees alongside the hawthorn hedge. I can't wait to tell Emma whom I wish to please.

The weather forecast is for two major incoming storms and dark clouds collapse over the Norfolk fenland. Lorries on the M11 stir up waves of water from the road. The cars look as if they are driving through dry ice. The river Wissey spills over the reeds and rushes, forming pools of water across the fields. The smaller roads are awash with water. The spray slaps the front windscreen. It is satisfying for the ten-year-old in all of us.

I stop for cat biscuits, frowning over the choices and packaging. And then I am home and clearing the hog house for its new resident. It is really so smart and substantial I cannot understood why it has been empty for so long. I send a picture on my phone to Emma with the caption: Peggy's home ready!

The response is doubtful. "Has that house got wire inside? Sorry to be a pain but if so it's unsuitable as they catch their feet on them. Have u got a wooden one? Or you can just build a wooden one."

I have a couple of goes at building a den from branches and leaves and my spirits lift when I get Emma's approval. I remind myself to think of the species rather than individuals but the truth is that Peggy is coming home.

Meanwhile, my parents' home remains empty. Their cleaner, Kate, still comes once a week. The beds are made; it is ready for them to step back through the door. But they are living in limbo, without a clear future and away from the beloved clutter of their past. I am torn between trying to make their nursing home rooms more homely and not wanting to imply that this is now their home.

I replace a generic picture of roses in my father's care home bedroom with one of a barn owl. I am not sure that he notices but it evokes him to those who come and go. I had tried a few other touches, such as rugs and cushions. But he slipped on the rug and fell and there is now an alarm-fitted rubber mat by his bed instead. When I go to see him, he is lying alert but unmoving on his bed. Too tired to read and in a place that voices on the radio can no longer reach.

When his friend, the vicar, Kit Chalcraft, suggested that he might like to hear some more of his beloved Beethoven, we looked for something simpler than even a radio. The technology taken for granted by the young can be miraculous for the old. My husband instals the voice recognition technology Alexa, and there is my dad, seraphic with pleasure, conducting from his bed Beethoven's *Pastoral Symphony*. I have also brought in photographs of my father and mother when they were young. They are living their marriage vows now, in sickness, for worse. The song of their early romance was "Some Enchanted Evening", from *South Pacific*, and I summon it for them from Alexa. They gaze at each other across an empty room, with the tender knowledge of a lifetime together.

The lines from T.S. Eliot's *Four Quartets* come to mind, as ever:

Time present and time past
Are both perhaps present in time future,
And time future contained in time past.

We don't talk of the future but we can guess what it is. We are just awaiting it, and my father does so with astonishing grace.

I put out the kitten biscuits and water by the new deluxe branch den and tear up rather superior pages from my husband's edition of *British Journalism Review*. The only box I can find with a lid once contained Coca Cola cans, which somehow seems bad brand advertising for a protected British species but it is too late to look for anything else. I set off towards King's Lynn at 4.30 and by the time I reach Emma's hedgehog hotel at 5.30 night is falling.

It is busy with cars parked haphazardly in the driveway or along the roadside as if we have discovered a little-known pub. Inside the hedgehog hospital, it is rather like Accident and Emergency. Thirty-one hedgehogs are being released this evening and Emma is at the centre of things, focused, her hair in a ponytail of fuchsia-pink satin.

Along the floor are rows of smart plastic travel crates, with neatly shredded lines from the *Daily Mail*. I try to slide my Coca Cola box behind my legs. A lithe-looking woman in the hedgehog demographic age group is dropping off and collecting. It turns out that she is Peggy's foster carer. But there has been some confusion and she has not brought Peggy. I say, oh, never mind, while trying to hide unexpectedly deep disappointment.

Emma is firm. Peggy must be released tonight. I ask only half jokingly if it is because of the full moon. Emma replies that the temperature is exactly right, about 12°C and Peggy is exactly the right weight. The release weight is 850 and she is 892. If we leave her any longer she will start to become stressed. I turn to the foster carer, Wendy, and offer to follow her home to pick up Peggy. She is in Hunstanton, on the Norfolk coast, about 18 miles from the hedgehog hospital.

She leaves with her new hedgehog, Anna Maria, and I follow her. We pass the Queen Elizabeth Hospital, from where I sprang my dad five months ago. It is now March 2022, and as we drive alongside Sandringham I hear on the radio news that Prince Andrew has settled his case with the American woman accusing him of sexual abuse. The Queen must be relieved. At least with hedgehogs all you have to worry about are maggots.

We arrive at Wendy's house and two collie dogs bound up to the front door. They and the hedgehogs have learned to rub along together.

Just outside the back door are the hedgehog cages, wooden and spacious. Wendy opens the door to a pile of hay and newspapers. She offers me some rubber gloves and I root around until I find a substantial ball of prickles. Before fat-shaming came along, a newspaper caption for Peggy's return might have read: "Piling on the pounds."

I lift her out and Wendy tries to take a photograph to send to Emma. But I cannot see her face or any features; the ball is closed. On Wendy's suggestion, I move her around a bit and I can feel her warm active weight. But she does not seem to have a face. Then Wendy tells me to turn her upside down. I flip her into the Coca Cola box and sure enough, there is the moist, dark snout and a padded paw, raised in the air like a royal wave. I exclaim but am not sure which epithets to use. Wendy and I know we are not to treat the hedgehogs as pets so cannot comment on their cuteness or other anthropomorphic qualities. I couldn't, for instance, comment that Peggy looks as if she could balance a cup of tea on her portly belly.

Neither must I ask if Wendy will miss Peggy after their months together. Friendships between humans and hedgehogs are not permitted.

So instead, I wave goodbye and in her fashion so does Peggy. And I place the box on the front passenger seat. We drive back to our home in what I would like to call companionable silence. There is not a sound from the box. Were the hedgehog a pet. I would have spoken to her, just to reassure her. I would tell her why we are on this moonlit road, past dusk now. I would have pointed out the lights from the houses in the villages, their kitchens and televisions creating a cosiness at odds with the darkness and rain outside. I would have tried to explain the emotional pull of home. Rescued hedgehogs are returned to the settings from which they came, but these are gardens, not houses. And while I can protect Peggy from pesticides or lawnmowers or (I have learned to my shame) pond nets, I cannot vouch for foxes and badgers or the shock of the semi-wild.

I turn the headlights on along the lane near our home to make sure that there is nothing on the road. It would be ironic to rescue one hedgehog only to drive over another. I see a hare and a few field mice. The ubiquitous roadkill in Norfolk is the pheasant, surviving the shooting season only to jay-walk country lanes.

We pull into our drive, I turn off the ignition and I look at Peggy, peering short-sightedly from her box. This is it. I put on the PPE gloves from the care home, take the box to the den by the hedge and shake her out.

Because it is dark I cannot observe her progress without shining a torch in her face. So I leave her to it.

That evening I luxuriate in homeliness. I have a deep bath, get into fresh Egyptian-cotton sheets and put my phone on silent. Before I go to sleep, I look out at the darkness, the silhouettes of trees, the high moon, shrouded in mist. And I remember that wildness is freedom.

Storm Dudley is whipping up the winds and the windows rattle and shake. The moon moves a spotlight into my bedroom through the gap in the curtains. I am restless thinking about Peggy out there in the night. Does her den of sticks feel like a home? Will she wander from it? I think of the damp beech leaves and the spread of aconites and snowdrops and the proximity of the hawthorn hedge. It is the most hedgehog-friendly landscape I can think of. There is a call of a tawny owl in the early hours and I look again from the window. I consider going out with a torch to check but can imagine Emma's disapproval if I start shining a light into the face of a wild mammal experiencing freedom for the first time in months.

I get back into bed, putting aside thoughts of the universe and Creation and philosophy in favour of human-scale mental to-do lists. I drift off only to be woken a couple of hours later by banging outside and footsteps. Half dreaming, I wonder if someone is after Peggy. I look out of the window. I am sure I heard a car but cannot see one. There are lights from the road and I shrug that it must be the acoustics of the storm. But then, no, I definitely hear more shouting, footsteps on the gravel, then inside the house. I freeze. Should I confront or hide? The clock says 4.50am which is surely an odd time for burglars. There is said to be a ghost in this house, a nun called Sister Barbara, who was walled up after consorting with highwaymen. But this is not the voice of a nun. It is a male voice, and the footsteps are coming up the stairs.

I turn the door handle at the same time as the intruder;

The Hedgehog Diaries

he is standing in front of me. It is my older brother. "You didn't answer your phone," he says. "And your downstairs window was open. Dad died in the night."

Obviously, we make a cup of tea. Then I get dressed, get into the car and turn on the headlights, and disappear down the drive. The darkness may be familiar to the hedgehog but it speaks of tumult, of birth or death, to the rest of us.

The night lights of the care home are calmly final. The head nurse on duty, Nadine, a great favourite of my dad's, opens the door, hugs me, leads me down the silent corridor and unlocks the bedroom door. My father lies on his side, his feathery white hair against the pillow, his features sculpted, his skin pale, his forehead cold. Yet, I can still lift and rub his hand. Not stiff yet, not gone yet. The window is open, for his spirit to leave.

By his bed is a copy of the Compline prayer. With unforeseen good timing, his friend the vicar had seen him the day before and they had discussed this prayer, read before nightfall, sleep a metaphor for death.

> Keep watch, dear Lord, with those who work, or watch, or weep this night, and give your angels charge over those who sleep. Tend the sick, Lord Christ; give rest to the weary, bless the dying, soothe the suffering, pity the afflicted, shield the joyous; and all for love's sake. Amen.

In the drawer by his bed is my father's notebook with

his scribbled thoughts, jotted down some months ago when he was still up to writing. His fears at "the end"; his doubts about the "afterlife". The writing was hurried and full of question marks. But the last sentence was one word. Compline. Perhaps an answer. As Rowan Williams said: acceptance is a form of faith.

The nurses are as quiet as nuns. They close the door behind them as they wash and dress him, choosing a checked shirt, removing his watch that he was never without, all done with quiet dignity, the ceremony of compassion.

I lead my mother to his bedside to say her farewell; the police and ambulance crew sit in the nurses' station filling out their certifications, muted, respectful. Then the stretcher goes into the bedroom and my father is carried out, covered by a maroon cloth, and I follow the undertaker with my sister and see that the nurses have formed a guard of honour along the corridor and reception area. As his body is lifted into the back of the hearse, a flock of rooks pass across the sky. Yes, there was something of St Francis about my dad.

My mother has had some brandy and is resting so I return home for a shower. I check the leaves and branches but cannot see the hedgehog. I walk around the boundary piles of leaves, check, logs and tree stumps and brambles and compost, check, check, check. But no hedgehog. The little bowl of water and kitten biscuits untouched. I look for any signs of badgers. I eye suspiciously the pheasant strutting across the lawn. I look across at the horses in the field. What do they know? The sound of flapping wings and a chorus of rooks rises from the branches of the lime trees.

At last spring came. The first warm day of the year, with a silvery south-west breeze, was the day of my father's funeral.

Dad had left behind more instructions for his funeral than I'd first thought and my brother put together an order of service that included the hymn "To be a Pilgrim" and ended with the ballad "Follow the Heron" which was to be played as the simple oak coffin, decorated with lilies and yew, was carried out by the grandsons.

My brother handed me a passage written by our father describing the departure of the pink-footed geese back to Iceland in late February. I was to read it to the music of Sibelius, the "swan" theme. The passage ran:

> I drove on to Titchwell. At least there would be a flock of lovely burnished golden plover to enjoy. But there, as I stopped in the car park, the sound of pinkfoot was deafening. Long before I could see them, loud as a film soundtrack, all around me, and so close!
>
> There were several thousand there already, on the field between sea path and village. I had never heard before this excited chatter, not here.
>
> Sometimes, they collect on the south side of the church and then, when they are ready they take

off as one, with a great whoosh of wings: twenty thousand birds or more, in a dark cloud which sets course for Holkham nine miles away.

But tonight, you could see the excitement, the nervousness and the tension in the flock. Every few minutes, one would rise, and the rest would follow, around the fields and the hill south of Titchwell and back to the Old Field Farm meadow. Not to rest or to feed but soon, very soon, in only hours, at dawn perhaps, to leave for their Icelandic paradise, into the sun, and out of sight, over the horizon.

Whatever instinct it is that drives these lovely birds to rise up into the air, and on MIGHTY wingbeats to cross the North Sea and then the Atlantic to fields unknown, it was driving them to a frenzy of excitement that day. And I too could feel it.

The lesson of funeral reading is to practise until the words harden and lose their power to make you choke.

Because my brother had been a chorister at Canterbury Cathedral, he was versed in funerals; he knew all about plain chant and how to compose an anthem. Liturgy and music wrap death in ceremonial balm. Funerals deserve the same attention as weddings yet the preparation is done in weeks and in muffled misery so we can be too hasty. Royals and Romanies know the value of a proper send-off.

Our godsend, appropriately, was the Rev Kit Chalcraft,

The Hedgehog Diaries

who was both friend to my dad and the boatman who rowed him to the other side. He officiated at a vigil the evening before and sat steadfast by the coffin. Funeral music cannot be condensed into a *Desert Island Discs*; the canon of musical history is too rich. My brother selected music to play through the night and for the service, and for the cremation. We bowed our heads in the vestry where the coffin lay, surrounded by candles and listened to Brahms: *A German Requiem*.

After the funeral service, in the civic blankness of the crematorium, the curtains closed around the coffin to the lucid, almost cheerful tones of Schubert's "Trout" Quintet. Fire and water.

At the end of the day, when all the guests had gone, Billy, my grandson, went to the front door of his home and looked searchingly out beyond the lawn to the woods and river. He called out: "Good night, Noel," and went back inside.

7

COMMUNITIES OF HEDGEHOGS – KIRTLINGTON AND SHROPSHIRE

On a bright, sharp, early spring morning, I drive to Shropshire to meet the hedgehog lady of Little Wenlock. I am starting to appreciate hedgehog country, and an activist village on the edge of the Shropshire hills has the ideal conditions. "A wilderness is rich with liberty," Wordsworth wrote. Hedgehogs like small places next to wide open spaces. Don't fence me in, as Cole Porter put it. No wonder they speak to our love of cottage gardens as well as fields beyond. Hedgehogs are on a human scale, if of a prehistoric lineage. I remember the hedgehog fact that they frown as a precursor to curling up. It is hard not to imagine them in caps and aprons when you think of this.

The human highway takes me up the M1 and M6 from industrial centres to a landscape of high hedgerows and soft yellow stone walls (pretty, but in the hedgehog world no good for escapes). I have agreed to meet Kathryn Jones at Little Wenlock's village hall but it turns out there is a dance class on, which the group leader tells me is being FILMED so we must shoo.

Instead, we find a bus shelter, and as the wind whistles through it, Kathryn shows me her hedgehog body of work: First-Class Honours dissertation, school packs, community guides and artwork of hedgehog prints.

She is 24 years old and has been a friend of wildlife since her childhood, a student of hedgehogs at college and is now an official hedgehog officer. She has an open face with wide grey-blue eyes and streaky blonde hair. She speaks with a mild intonation of her native Wolverhampton and carries a rucksack imprinted with pictures of hedgehogs and a hedgehog toy dangling from it.

When she applied for her role at Shropshire Wildlife Trust, they told her that the only thing more she could have done would have been to dress up as a hedgehog. If you cut her in half (a horrid, badger-like image), you would find her hedgehog-hearted. Her father and brother work for West Midland trains, and her sister is a tattoo artist but Kathyn's vocation was never in doubt. "I fell in love with hedgehogs," she says with a shrug.

You can see her influence on Little Wenlock. Outside the village hall is a sign strapped to the telegraph pole: "Slow Hedgehogs Please Drive Carefully Thank You". The hedgehog lady of Little Wenlock has issued residents with a ten-point plan:

* Link your garden.
* Keep a wild area.
* Do not disturb hibernating hogs.
* Check before mowing.
* Make a log pile.
* Do not use pesticides.
* Keep ponds safe.
* Tie up garden netting [I blush with shame].
* Do not drop litter.
* Log your hog.

For Kathryn, this is a mission rather than a job. She tries to explain which bits she gets paid for. Her trips to primary schools to teach children how to make clay hedgehogs and houses from moss and sticks earn her a living. Most of the children will not have seen a hedgehog in real life; they rely on the older generation to describe them. Patrolling New Wenlock, Kathryn does her road-kill count. "Church lane is where you see them, cars come past at speed," she says. House visits tend to be more cheering. Along quiet neat lanes, wheelie bins are parked at the ends of drives with their communal messages: Slow Hedgehogs.

We turn down the drive of a retired couple, whose property in Kathryn's eyes is a model home. The couple are not here but they have left clues. Through the living-room window, I can see an almost complete 1000-piece jigsaw of a barn owl. In the garden shed at the back is a draughtsperson's table and watercolours of characters from Beatrix Potter, of mushrooms and birds. The people who live here adhere to Gilbert White's dictum about observing narrowly.

The half-an-acre-or-so garden itself is exemplary: paths, little ponds with ramps, fern areas, vegetable beds, piles of logs, wild areas and at least two hibernating houses with arched wooden entrances and stones for roofs. Once you have seen a hedgehog-friendly environment like this, you became aware of the paved, sterile, bricked-up indifference of so many new developments.

Hedgehog lady says she will continue her patrols and ministry in the hope that more people will open their hearts and their gardens. "We have gone from 30 million hedgehogs to less than a million. They are declining faster than tigers are worldwide." She is momentarily disheartened: "I am doing my best but it will be up to the young people to save the hedgehog." This, after less than a decade of adulthood.

Two days later, I spot some good news in the papers. We may be on the brink of war with Russia but on page 9 of *The Times*, that symbol of Nato, the hedgehog, has the promise of a new status. The government is planning on upgrading protections for British wildlife. There are pictures of a red squirrel and a hedgehog. The government has set a target to stop species decline by 2030. The article tells us that "the British hedgehog population in the countryside has more than halved since 2000". I make a note to try the Radio 4 statistics programme *More or Less* on the veracity of these numbers but meanwhile I send the news to Kathryn. She responds: "That's great news" and in celebration sends me nocturnal camera footage of two hedgehogs mating like steam trains and a fox pressing its nose against a hedgehog and backing off.

Hedgehog activism among the young is striking. I find online two thirteen-year-old schoolgirls called Kyra Barboutis and Sophie Smith who have campaigned to turn their area of Stratford-upon-Avon into a Hedgehog Friendly Town. The pair have fought against netting on trees and hedgerows, calling to account the housing developers Taylor Wimpey who, upon meeting the girls, removed the netting. These Greta Thunbergs of biodiversity can use their social media following to change policy. If Taylor Wimpey back down in the face of social media videos, governments must be next.

I am also testing my theory about the good nature and capacity for joy among those who look after hedgehogs. A few weeks after seeing Kathryn Jones, I seek out the Surrey branch of the Wildlife Trust and particularly Elizabeth Foster, a local hedgehog champion. She is catching up in the office after a village hall meeting the evening

The Hedgehog Diaries

before, at Riverhead, near Sevenoaks, her beat extending from Surrey to Kent. I remember the place from my days as a local newspaper reporter on the *Sevenoaks Chronicle*. I drove my battered green van to cover parish council meetings, flower shows, golden wedding anniversaries and police and fire calls. Let us say that these were not mean streets. There was one spectacular murder, which brought Fleet Street down to the local pub with their large expense accounts and demands for my contacts book. And there were periodic pile-ups caused by fog on the M20. Otherwise, my shorthand notebook was full of faithful recordings of planning applications for conservatories.

I would have liked to have gone back with my notebook for Lizzie's meeting about the state of hedgehog infrastructure in Riverhead and surrounding areas. She reported back to me that there was an audience of about 30, described as " older", about half of whom had spotted hedgehogs. They other half had not, but remembered seeing them in their younger lives.

On Zoom, Lizzie has a lively face, and lifts up a mug, which reads "Beware, hedgehog crazy lady". She does not seem crazy, just strikingly content. Aged 28, she has discovered that being among hedgehogs – and her other great love, bats – puts her in harmony with the world. She never tires of hedgehogs; spotting them, saving them, weighing them. She still finds them "charismatic" and individual. There is so much more to find out about them. For instance, she says, a local resident sent her some footage of a hedgehog at a feeding station biffing another hedgehog out of the way. "I have never seen that behaviour before," she says.

She is so curious and kindly that I blurt out my fears for Peggy, the hedgehog that I have released and apparently lost. What does she think might have happened to her?

"Just because you can't see them doesn't mean they aren't there," she says, a gentle possibility that I have repeated to myself since.

Then she adds: "Remember they travel up to two miles, so may have found a road."

My heart sinks again.

The population of hedgehogs in East Anglia is dangerously low, not helped by me. Big open fields, fewer hedgerows, use of pesticides.

But in Surrey, things are looking up. Lizzie says that the landscape is more appealing, with small farms, woodland and an educated human population who understand that every garden needs an escape hole. It is a county of connectivity and so hedgehog numbers are increasing.

Lizzie has the young and the old on side, but is concerned about losing teenagers to technology. They are less interested in the outdoors. When she talks to them about hedgehogs, their main reference is Sonic the Hedgehog.

Lizzie believes that the mental health epidemic that hit the young during lockdown could have been assuaged if they had had a greater communion with nature. She rents a cottage on a farm that has all that she, and a hedgehog, should need. Log piles, a pond, a compost heap. She says it was the butterflies that got her through lockdown. And just breathing in and out in fresh air.

Now it is approaching spring, the dawn chorus is becoming more exuberant; the rhythms of the day more pronounced. I wish my dad could see the blossom and the daffodils, but then perhaps he still can. Just because I can't see him doesn't mean he is not there.

Lizzie's observation that semi-rural hedgehogs are doing better than rural ones is supported by The State of Britain's Hedgehogs 2022 report, from the British Hedgehog Preservation Society. The rural populations are still in sharp decline, most notably in the East of England. But in more urban areas, with hedgehog activism, the populations are stabilising. I find now that walking down the street I instinctively check for escape routes in walls and fences. I raise it at a board meeting for Berkeley Group, the home builders. In a year that could do with some cheering news to counter the doomscrolling, we may have alighted on it.

In 2020, hedgehogs were put on the Red List by the International Union for Conservation for Nature, as vulnerable to extinction in the UK. But green spaces in urban places may save them. The surveys do not provide exact data, because, as Lizzie has reassured me, hedgehogs can be hard to find. In 2018, the Mammal Society estimated the hedgehog population of the UK to be 879,000. While they are doing better in urban areas, they are also more likely to be squashed on the roads. Ten to 20 per cent of hedgehog losses each year are road deaths.

It is just over a decade since Hedgehog Street was launched to create hedgehog communities and a hedgehog map of the UK. It records its progress in numbers: 100,000 hedgehog champions; more than one million signatures to the government demanding that new housing developments incorporate hedgehog highways; 16,000 hedgehogs highways created. The British are expressing on a grand scale the sentiment of Ted Hughes: "I don't know why I am so sympathetic towards hedgehogs."

The most sympathetic village of all to hedgehogs must be Kirtlington in Oxfordshire.

The scene is daffodils and blizzards on my pre-Easter visit to this model village. "There are no fuck-off gates here," says Chris Powles, financial investor, Kenyan conservationist, but known here by the village children as "hedgehog man".

Kirtlington is near Oxford and the village bursts with rectories and professors. There are two pubs (one currently closed) and one post office (currently closed), but a thriving Church of England school, a village hall and a well-organised parish council, kept in shape by Chris's wife, Ruth, who is the parish clerk. The greyish-yellow Oxfordshire stone-and-slate village has at its centre a village pond and a church. Magnolia trees blossom in emerald front lawns. When Chris built the hedgehog hole into the churchyard, he consulted his wife on suitable building materials. She prescribed weathered oak. As luck would have it, there was a fallen wonky oak sign to the church, which Chris used as a kind of doorframe around the hedgehog entrance. Hedgehogs now enter the graveyard under the piece of wood that reads: Church.

Chris has a desk with tidy piles of documents relating to his renewable energy investments, both here and on the Zambezi river. But his shelves are full of titles published by the Mammal Society; his screensavers on his two laptops are of elephants from his Mount Elgon conservation site in Kenya, and hedgehogs from his back garden.

On a wooden surface are cards depicting hedgehogs, sent by the children of Kirtlington, and a mug of a hedgehog holding a banner saying "hedgehogs need help". One of the card writers appeared on the BBC's *One Show* to talk about the Kirtlington community project, a small item following the centrepiece star guest Dolly Parton. The country-and-western singer was so tickled by the hedgehog scheme that Kirtlington's cameo role expanded before the eyes of bemused producers.

Chris, a work-from-home financier, bespectacled in a fleece and jeans, understands what makes him happy: the beautiful formal garden outside his window (his pride is ambivalent because "formal" can be a derogatory word in the hedgehog community); the craftsmanship of the hedgehog holes he has created for his garden and those of his neighbours, which he likens to Stonehenge; chopping wood; and the knowledge as he falls asleep that there will be nocturnal activity far away among the elephants in the Kenyan bush and nearby among hedgehogs at his feeding station.

The feeding station is a feat of engineering. It is an arrangement of bricks with a slate roof, creating two entrances/exits. It is too low to allow cats and foxes inside and the sharp right angle of bricks creates a further barrier inside the corridor. I think sadly of my bowls and kitten biscuits left out for Peggy and enjoyed by the neighbourhood cat. Sometimes your best is not good enough.

The hedgehog man of Kirtlington is rewarded for his ingenuity. He shows me on his laptop his nocturnal camera footage from the previous night. A delicate female enters the feeding station, glides on long legs past the right angle down the corridor and reaches the bowls of food and water. Minutes later, a brute of a male squeezes himself along the same route, elongating his body to get past the corner. A few more meals, and he might have got stuck.

Chris's most famous construction is for a couple, Zoe and Peter Kyte, who lives in an elegant white house with a slate roof, with a view of a beautiful informal garden leading to a pond. There had been just one barrier for hedgehogs – the height discrepancy with the neighbouring wall – but Chris had got round this by making an elevated hedgehog hole and a steep ramp.

Zoe, a barrister, is slender and girlish and confined to a wheelchair. She says that she knows about ramps and this is an impressive one. The photograph of one of the first hedgehogs to make its way down, taken by Chris's brother, Stephen Powles, a wildlife photographer, became

The Hedgehog Diaries

a social media hit. The village became famous outside the world of hedgehogs.

Chris's hedgehog devotion began around six years ago, a Wind in the Willows final chapter in a wildlife journey that began in his Kenyan childhood. His grandfather was of a different age, a farmer who shot elephants and then became a conservationist. His passion was for the Troglodyte elephants in the caves of Mount Elgon National Park. His father was in the East African newspaper business. When the Brits cleared out in 1969, after the white farms were sold off, Chris's family moved to the London suburbs, where his father died shortly afterwards. It was his grandfather who taught him that British birds can be as fascinating as the more vivid African varieties.

He shows me a portrait of a bird in flight which is so dynamic and charismatic that I express surprise, when, on close inspection, I see it is only a robin. "Only?" says Chris, frowning.

I flinch at disappointing him and also feel the pained response of my father. I have been learning that the being of someone you love does not cease with their death. My mother finds herself wanting to pass on information to my father and experiencing genuine aftershocks on realising that he is not there. As Philip Larkin put it in his poem about the hedgehog killed by his mower: "Next morning I got up and it did not. The first day after a death, the new absence is always the same…"

I continue a mental one-sided dialogue with Dad. Look how the blossom is out on the crab apple trees you bought me. Here is the first frogspawn in the pond we created in Norfolk. Our continued conversation must embrace disapproval as well as approval. He would have been as dismayed as Chris at my lack of proper dues for the robin.

Like Chris, my father had been in East Africa for some years, but never disparaged the more muted appeal of British birds. He always saw distinctions between the little brown jobs. I would have emailed him the article that appeared after his death in the *Telegraph* with the headline: "Scientists ruffle feathers by proving British birds are dull".

A Sheffield university study published in April 2022 showed that British birds are almost a third less vibrant than those in tropical climes. The greater variety of food sources in rainforests and other biodiverse environments encouraged birds to become vainer about their appearances. British birds struggling to survive in cooler temperatures could not worry about these fripperies. They are yeomen rather than courtiers.

We have to appreciate the subtleties of native appearance and character, with a twitchery excitement about migration. I learned from my father that a bird in the wrong place is a news event. Observe narrowly and appreciate what is in front of you.

For those who succumb to wildlife enthusiasm, each day is a discovery. The village's swift specialist wanders in with news of the Cherwell colony, which gather under eaves. Come May, the swifts will be everywhere. For Chris

Powles, hedgehog man, it is the connection between Kenya and Kirtlington, his heart, on the wing.

But my main reason for coming to see Chris is that he is the sleuth of Kirtlington, He has written a seminal paper on one of the great unsolved mysteries of the hedgehog world: what happened to the hedgehogs of Kirtlington during lockdown?

The report has an irresistible title:

Community of Kirtlington and the mystery of the lockdown hedgehogs.

Kirtlington – mid-Oxfordshire parish of around 460 properties and 1000 hedgehog enthusiasts, as members of the Kirtlington Wildlife and Conservation Society.

Report by Christopher Powles, Kirtlington Wildlife and Conservation Society

In May 2020 there was a sudden and near total disappearance of hedgehogs from Kirtlington.

May 5. Household 3 emailed author expressing concern that no hedgehog had visited for about two weeks.

May 6. Household 4 emailed author that "a week ago" they had found a dead hedgehog in their garden and that a badger had appeared on their camera trap eating food meant for the hedgehog.

May 15. Household 1 recorded first night with no hedgehogs on its camera trap.

May 15. Household 2 reported a reduction in activity from probably four or more to probably only two hedgehogs.

May 19. Household 5 recorded its last night with a hedgehog.

June 1. Household 2 reported a reduction to only one hedgehog from probably two.

June 6. Household 2 recorded its last night with a hedgehog.

Busy with babies?

Thirst/hunger – dry weather could have taken the earthworms.

Disease: none known of.

Poisoning by slug pellets?

Change of human behaviour? People started using gardens more, staying out in the evenings.

Foxes? No remains.

Badgers: were present and chief suspects.

Unseasonal weather.

Covid lockdown: less roadkill for scavengers, so maybe they came searching gardens.

Badgers! Multiple sightings on camera traps.

Clue: hedgehog remains. "The skin and prickles remains" referred to by household 4 is characteristic of how badgers eat hedgehogs, i.e. they open them up when curled up with powerful claws, place them on their backs and eat them from underneath.

Patrick Doncaster, Professor of Ecology at the School of Biological Sciences at the University of Southampton, studied hedgehogs in Kirtlington Park in 1992. He showed hedgehogs' preference for mown grass of lawns and playing fields. And that the concentration of hedgehogs was inverse to the concentration of badgers – two of his study animals were eaten, one by a badger and one by a dog.

Given the affection in which hedgehogs are held by many (including the author!) and the considerable effort expended by many in the village to promote hedgehogs, the sudden and near total decline of the village's hedgehog population is a matter of great upset. Some of the resulting comment in village social media can even be described as emotive. However, it is important not to jump to conclusions, to examine what evidence exists for what has happened and remember that "nature is nature". In the opinion of the author such evidence as there is does point to badgers. The skin and prickles were found at the home of criminal barrister Zoe Lyte.

"Was it the badgers?" I ask Chris. He answers with more scientific reservation than in his original paper. "Badgers certainly ate one. I would have expected to find more skin and prickles and for there to have been more badger sightings in the village."

The year the hedgehogs disappeared from Kirtlington will go down in parish history.

Stephanie, a wildlife conservationist who shows me around the village, is on the side of the badgers, believing that they get a bad press. She is indignant about the farmer-led badger cull on grounds that they may carry TB. The stewardship of the countryside is full of little conflicts of interest.

When I use the approved measurement of species, roadkill, for example, to surmise that there are many more pheasants and badgers in East Anglia than there are hedgehogs, Chris makes an immediate causal link. The grandson of a man who shot elephants is not against shooting pheasants but he worries that the breeding of them for shooting has its impact on hedgehogs. Too many pheasants, too few insects to go round.

Later he shows he me around his formal/informal gardens and alights on some specimen hedgehog poo. This is its own area of study, as I have already learned from Emma's hedgehog hospital in Norfolk. The poo that inspires Chris are the drops that shimmer with the skin of beetles. He puts some on a stick and smells it appreciatively before inviting me to do the same. We are suddenly nosing. The insight I can manage is to say that it is definitely unlike fox poo. It smells fresh and grassy. Apparently only surpassed by otter poo, which smells of Earl Grey and jasmine.

Here we are in the middle of an Oxfordshire village, in sunshine and snow showers, having a highly refined discussion about the scents of faeces. I could not be happier. Stephanie says that the eloquence of natural wildlife enthusiasts speaks to the character of Kirtlington. In the churchyard is the gravestone of Hugh Geoffroy Millain, the 20th-century British author, adventurer and actor. His inscription reads: "He was born with a gift of laughter and a sense that the world was mad."

8

GRIEF, FAITH, HOPE AND HEDGEHOGS

As Emma from the hedgehog hospital said, there is something magical about hedgehogs, something almost unicorn-like. I have a television executive friend who once threw a stone at what he thought was a rat moving outside his kitchen only to find he had killed a hedgehog. He felt a shiver of horror, as if he must be cursed for it. The peaceful but mysterious hedgehog makes us think of our patch of land and beyond it; we can study and protect them but we cannot hold onto them. Over the hill and far away they go.

The Hedgehog Diaries

My friend Jane Byam Shaw was brought up as a nature lover and she passed this on to her small son Felix. From the time they moved to north Oxford at the start of this century, Felix started putting up camera traps in the garden. As soon as he woke up, he would run out into the garden in his pyjamas to retrieve the memory stick. At school, he and his classmates would make clay hedgehogs together, and Jane's home became a clearing house for sick hedgehogs which she and Felix would drive to their local hedgehog hospital.

Like Beatrix Potter, the Byam Shaws had moved from London, and Felix was captivated by rural dusk, shining his torchlight into the bushes in the hope of finding a hedgehog. And the hedgehogs came.

His mother says Felix had an instinct for seeing the natural world. It was a kind of superpower. He would spot deer in Port Meadow before anyone else could. Rather like Beatrix Potter, he was attentive to rabbits.

In the summer of 2014, when Felix was 14 years old, he went on holiday to France with family friends and did not return. He died of a rare form of meningitis. In Jane's final desperate phone conversation with him as the severity of his sudden illness became apparent, he sounded confused and blurry and wanted to come home. A mother's heart cracked.

Jane, her husband Justin and their elder son Dan buried Felix in Woodeaton, Oxford, and Jane likes to think that rabbits play there.

Jane is not religious but she understands how nature is

a form of faith. She describes a spiritual experience during the bottomless darkness of the days following Felix's death. It was a memorably hot summer and she would lie on her son's bed looking blankly at the open window.

She says: "I suddenly noticed a butterfly on my arm in bed, in the room, and it was so odd because in the weeks after that the butterflies kept appearing. I kept finding butterflies in his room."

One day, Jane went with her husband to look at the plot where Felix would be buried, and as they were walking away, she saw a butterfly resting on the exact spot chosen for the grave.

She sends me a photograph that she had taken in her garden soon after her son's death. "23 August, 2014 – just over a month after Felix died". A butterfly nestles on her arm. She says: "I have never known one land before and it felt like a sign. I am not superstitious but these things were unmistakeable."

Then came the hedgehogs. Jane remembers a hummingly hot summer afternoon sitting in the shade of the kitchen with her husband and his stepbrother; looking out of the window he pointed out a mole in the middle of the lawn. When Jane went to look she saw that it was a hedgehog, wobbly and confused in the blazing heat of the day. Jane took it to the hedgehog hospital, as she had taken many before with Felix, and once again she took it as a sign. "It was something I had done with Felix and I started to think: what could I do for hedgehogs?"

For Jane, the natural world kept her son close and gave

her a path through her mourning.

"It connected me to neighbours: you tend to get reclusive and it did give me a reason to talk to people and it was something Felix's friends liked to be involved in."

I think of Rory Stewart's claim that nobody is going to have a punch-up with you on social media on the topic of hedgehogs. Jane found that the bridges and open doors that allow hedgehogs to wander freely were metaphorical as well as literal. She sought advice from Hugh Warwick, who suggested that she needed a patch the size of two golf courses to do anything meaningful. So she consulted her Google map, and drew a boundary, which included two Oxford colleges and the banks of the Cherwell.

Then she bought a massive power drill to set about the thick brick walls of Oxford gardens and she got to work, setting up hedgehog highways through her patch of the City. And in the process, she talked to neighbours, discovered communities of both old and young, and immersed herself in the natural world.

Jane says that she realised helping hedgehogs helped everything else.

"The nice thing about hedgehogs is that they are a bellweather: anything you do for hedgehogs, including leaving wild patches in your garden, helps all wildlife. You can help all of nature by looking after hedgehogs."

Felix's empathy with the natural world was part of a wider compassion he felt for those who were unlucky. And so Jane and Justin Byam Shaw set up together the Felix food project, taking leftover food from shops and restaurants and delivering it in bright-green vans emblazoned with the Felix logo to food banks and shelters.

While I can always look back at the finished jigsaw of my father's life, Jane does not know what Felix would have done had he lived an adult life, but she thinks he would certainly have combined conservation of nature with helping others. So that, through his parents, is his legacy.

On the last anniversary of Felix's death, Jane was driving to Dorset, where she and Justin had been working on a rewilding project. Suddenly, the car in front of her stopped for no reason. She braked and peered out of her window.

She says: "I realised the car was letting a hedgehog cross the road – then I found a hedgehog in our walled garden in Dorset a day later, so I attach this Felix aura to them. I think he is sending me hedgehogs."

I ask tentatively if this amounts to faith, and Jane hesitates. I can see that a mother who loses a child might question the beneficence of God.

"Felix was born on Good Friday, which always felt a bit weird, as if that affected his destiny."

So while she cannot believe in God in the Church sense, she feels the spiritual dimension and Felix's place in it.

Her elder son, Dan, walked the length of Crete the Easter after Felix died. He had studied Greek Lament at Oxford and his thoughts on grief and the afterlife have become a memoir of loss.

For Jane, the spiritual realm is the natural world. "If

we don't care about losing hedgehogs we lose our moral compass. There is a morality, an innate call inside me, to do something if I can." For example, helping others. "The act of saving food and the environment is a sort of spiritual act, something about thankfulness for food and making it go round feels like a religious theme."

As my brother wrote to my father before he died: *Proficiscere, anima Christiana.*

In his work on grief and faith, C.S. Lewis described his state of mind after the death of his wife: "There is a sort of invisible blanket between the world and me." As for God, it is as if "there are no lights in the windows". The author asks the question: "Why has thou forsaken me?"

The conventional phrase we use when addressing the bereaved is to say that we are sorry "for your loss". Where death comes early and suddenly, loss feels too small a word to describe the existential wound.

In July 2019, Ben Goldsmith and Kate Rothschild's 15-year-old daughter Iris was killed in an off-road vehicle accident. Ben has written a book about his journey of grief and how it opened a vista into faith.

Ben, who is 41, comes from a family of landed environmentalists. Looking at his Instagram, you might settle on the word "charmed". Here he is watching cricket with Mick Jagger, or on a Caribbean beach at sunset, or beside a campfire at his farm in Somerset. His wife, Jemima, is beautiful and their small children enchanting. There was no obvious need for consolation until his daughter Iris died and the invisible blanket separated him from the world. As with Jane Byam Shaw, nature was the guide, if not the saviour.

Ben's London home is in Barnes, admirable for its trees and common hedgehog infrastructure, and he remembers walking with his daughter through the verdant graveyard by the little church of St Mary's, never imagining that he would be burying her there a month later.

In the aftermath of her death, he was in a state of blind shock. He withdrew to his farm in Somerset and wondered how he could live.

He says: "I found myself blinking in the immediate aftermath of Iris's death – I don't know if you have experienced deep trauma but it is a feeling of terror. It is a fear that waxes and wanes but never goes away – you learn some tricks for managing it.

"I found myself early on wandering shellshocked down to the pond at my place in Somerset – I stripped down and dived and I remember swimming deep and curling into a ball, then bobbing back up, blinking in the sunlight. And I was surrounded by dragonflies hovering above the water, butterflies and swallows and house martins skimming the water to drink and the sun was in shafts through the clouds and it was a beautiful moment, and I remember having consciously the thought that the world is very beautiful and it wasn't lost on me."

Was the beauty painful? I wondered.

Ben, who has a soft, unhurried delivery, replies: "In that moment it was a sense of surprise that the world was more piercingly, movingly beautiful than ever. I felt this sense of being held, of being carried. At the moment you most need it, God is there for you. I felt that as a physical experience."

He describes the momentary silencing of the pain, in a setting thrumming with natural life, both benign and indifferent.

Jane Byam Shaw sensed that butterflies were messengers from Felix. Ben saw rainbows on clear days, and sometimes just as he and his children were talking about Iris. The name Iris means rainbow. Then there were the birds that flew into the house in the days after Iris died.

"We had birds, lots of them, coming into the house. It was unusual, I don't remember it happening before but then in a space of week it must have happened about eight times; a house martin, a pigeon – extraordinarily tame, I am open-minded to it all."

Meanwhile, some of Iris's many pets – her rabbits, guinea pigs, a young cat – simply lay down and died. "I am glad to think that they are with her."

Her pony survived and sometimes Iris's father would stroke its muzzle and whisper: "Has she been to see you? Has she?"

Before Iris's death, Ben had considered nature to be wholly separate from faith. Afterwards, he became sympathetic towards a "spiritual realm". He visited a medium, a monk, a rabbi and a vicar, and took the psychedelic drug ayahuasca.

But it was nature that gave him his purpose and

solace. Ben shows me an early Instagram video that Iris sent him. There is her 13-year-old voice, youthful, outdoors, amazed, laughing. She is filming a murmuration at the bottom of the field. Her voice is caught by the wind: "Look! They are going up! Look how giant that is! I was right next to them!"

As Pascal put it in *Pensées*, those of faith always try to prove the existence of God from the works of nature… "yet it is a remarkable fact that no canonical writer has ever used Nature to prove God".

Nature the solace, nature the purpose. And the hedgehog one of the key indicators that the depletion of nature in the United Kingdom is being reversed.

Ben's brother is Lord Goldsmith, the Environment Minister. In the week in April in which Russia launches a fresh assault on eastern Ukraine and the Prime Minister is subject to a parliamentary inquiry over parties in Downing Street, I make my claim on behalf of hedgehogs in a phone call with him.

The peer is canny enough to spot the Red Wall, Red Meat backlash against "eco zealots" as energy costs soar; he talks of nature rather than climate. As for hedgehogs, they are the true reconcilers. The great writer and hedgehog enthusiast Tom Holland recently advised shy green Conservatives that nobody can feel emotional about carbon targets but if the Government came out with hedgehog targets the nation would rally. Zac Goldsmith says: "There would be no division between left and right because everyone cares about hedgehogs."

I put to him the notion from Rowan Williams that the hedgehog might be an Aslan figure. The sign of spring returning to a country healthy and at peace is a sighting of hedgehogs. Could not the hedgehog, symbol of Nato, make a fitting symbol for the UK? "I love that," says Zac.

While one crisis follows another in public life, the public themselves are now basking in the April sunshine, gathering in the liberty of large numbers in parks or walking in woodland and along rivers. Wild cherry and hawthorn follow the early blackthorn. The pair of crab apple trees in my garden, a present from my father, resemble his great white head on a pillow. I have never seen the blossom so snowy.

Hedgehogs mean hope. And Zac Goldsmith says we should nurture them. "It does not take that much effort." He has watched how the hedgehog population in Barnes has shot up after two local people, a Belgian jeweller and a burly electrician, created superhighways through the London village. Highways and habitat are the answer.

"If you shave every inch of grass and douse it in chemicals you are not going to have hedgehogs." Hedgehogs needs hedges. They are corridors, brimming with insect life.

While the government rushes out initiatives to placate its backbenches, another Wind in the Willows plan is taking place at a different pace: 1000 km of river regeneration. You can measure England through its networks of water. A grand coalition of interests has joined forces:

Natural England, the Beaver Trust, the chalk stream enthusiasts, the lovers of otters and brown trout and water voles, of kingfishers and mayflies. I think of Mole in *Wind in the Willows* "intoxicated with the sparkle, the ripple, the scents and the sounds and sunlight, he trailed a paw in the water and dreamed long waking dreams."

Lord Goldsmith asks: "Who doesn't like walking alongside water instead of a bleak desert?"

I recall what Professor Stephanie Holt from the Natural History Museum said. Have we underappreciated British wildlife, somehow looking elsewhere to the exoticism of African safaris rather than at what is in front of us?

Zac says sadly: "We have taken it for granted for decades and what is out of sight is out of mind. How many young people today have seen a wild hedgehog? But as a child I used to see them and feed them. If a child would see a hedgehog appear in their garden or a patch of green, wherever it is, it would be just so exciting. This has become a country where we think that nature is something that happens somewhere else."

He tells me of a visit from a Colombian colleague to Knepp Wildland, the regenerative farm project begun by Isabella Tree. The Colombian lived in the Amazon. Lord Goldsmith told her that Knepp was our equivalent. "This speck on the map, this oasis of diversity."

Lord Goldsmith must return to parliamentary business but he says before he leaves: "I know I am a zealot but it seems to me that whatever the question, the answer always come back to nature."

9

HIBERNATION, SLEEP AND BLONDE BOMBSHELLS

Spring is in its full regalia; the birds in the branches are blasting out their Hallelujah Chorus and the early swifts are returning and breeding. Dark winter is over and the garden is bathed in bright April light, and I am conscious of leaving my dad behind. He died in the gloom of late February, the Compline prayer by his side: "The Lord Almighty grant us a quiet night and a perfect end."

The sleep of the grave.

Our grandson Billy had innocently expressed that

double meaning when he stood on the doorstep after the funeral wake and called out across the lawn to the horizon: "Good night, Noel."

When I had asked Dad how he felt during the winter months he said: "Oh, you know, sleepy and idle. I don't feel I am much use to anybody." I replied that I preferred to see it as a storing-up of strength, a preservation of energy, a kind of hibernation. I was hopeful, but Dad was faithful.

He would have thought of spring as Kenneth Grahame did of human progress: "A new world is being born... And one cannot grieve for the old, the new is all so wonderful."

Hibernation is an extraordinary state: more than sleep, less than death. It is a suspended state. A kind of voluntary coma. It is a mystery to me, but, by a piece of luck, my husband Kim happens to mention a conversation he had with a dinner companion at an Oxford college event. Dr Vladyslav Vyazovskiy, who gave grace in Ukrainian, is Associate Professor of Neuroscience at the Department of Physiology, Anatomy and Genetics at Oxford.

He has written a paper on sleep, in which he reminds us that we sleep through a third of our lives. It is a state of otherness: "When we fall asleep, it is not only that the world ceases to exist for us, but, figuratively speaking, we also take a leave of absence, and effectively stop existing, from the outer world's perspective."

And we share this state with the natural world. "We live on a half-asleep planet."

A couple of days later, I am happily on Zoom with

Vlad, with his bowl-shaped sheen of brown hair and a curious smile, discussing the state of hibernation in Siberian mice, its implication for sending people to Mars, and the philosophical distinctions between existing – consciousness – and death.

I think again of Compline and the process of dying. In the case of my father, I guess his faint heart gave way and his breathing stopped. Did he know that he was dying, or was he unaware of it?

Vlad directs me to a book by Evan Thompson called *Waking, Dreaming, Being* and research by the Centre for Healthy Minds at the University of Wisconsin-Madison. It examines the Tibetan Buddhist traditions on postmortem meditative states. Medical science makes a distinction between the state of life and death but it is more complicated when some bodily functions can be kept artificially present. In my father's case, the doctor had said his heart only continued to operate because of drugs; what then of those on ventilators? The signs of life we acknowledge are the heart beating, breathing, and brain activity.

In some religions, the line between life and death is less clear. Death, writes Evan Thompson, may not be "an event that occurs as a single point in time". Tibetan Buddhists believe in a state called Tukdam, accessible in the act of dying. According to the University of Wisconsin-Madison's research: "All humans are said to have this opportunity as it is believed to arise naturally during the process of dying but only advanced meditators are thought to have the ability to apprehend and use that experience for spiritual realisation."

The author attends a meditative session on the experience of dying, led by a Buddhist teacher named Roshi Joan. She says that the process of falling asleep closely resembles what happens when you die. Your sensory grip on the world is loosening. "As your body slips away", she says, "the outside world slips away too… This is the dissolution of the earth element as form unbinds into feelings."

"At the moment of so-called physical death, Roshi Joan described a small, flickering flame like a candle. Suddenly, it's extinguished and your awareness is gone."

I think of the vigil for my father that my brother had prepared in the church. Dad's coffin surrounded by candles in the darkness. Flickering candles a friendly companion in the unknown.

Roshi Joan then guides the author into the next stage.

"A deep black sky, free of stars or moon appears. Out of this nothingness, luminescence arises. You are one with clear dawn sky free of sunlight, moonlight and darkness. You are bliss and clarity."

This state of radiance prolongs a kind of consciousness beyond the point of death, and among those who are spiritually liberated it can ward off physical decomposition for weeks.

It is a common observation that those close to death become mentally much clearer and calmer. We call it remission but it may be a spiritual opportunity. My father's friend, Kit Chalcraft, who visited him on his last afternoon, remarked to my mother as he left the room that my father seemed much more lucid than in previous visits. What did this presage?

The person with whom I would most have loved to talk about this, died that night. When I saw him the following morning and stroked his cold forehead and held his not yet stiff hand, he had crossed into death. But was it a process or a moment? Is self or consciousness a process?

Every time Dad pops up on my iPhone photo memories, I will him back. Can the strength of my memories connect to a posthumous consciousness? Where is he? All I can think is that he is in the natural world and that is where I will find him. I understand now his wish to be cremated rather than buried.

> At the round earth's imagined corners blow
> Your trumpets, angels, and arise, arise,
> From death, our numberless infinities
> Of souls and to your scattered bodies go..
> John Donne, Holy Sonnet VII

Vlad is open-minded about the Buddhist notion of a process of dying rather than a death, but he has a different scientific mission. He wants to study hibernation, or as he calls it, the state of torpor – extreme conservation of energy in order to survive, because if human beings are going to get to Mars, they are going to have to learn to switch off.

He frowns as he does the maths: "How long to get to Mars? Seven hundred days. Shortest is 450 days, longest more than 1000. It is a very long time."

Hibernation means that you do not eat or drink, you do not defecate, you do not breathe oxygen. You are also protected from cosmic radiation because the speed of chemical reactions slows down. You are going to be in much better shape.

The 57th Astronautical Congress examined this and concluded:

> During the time-consuming transfer to the final goal of an interplanetary mission, only minimal if any human activity and control will be required. As a consequence it would be desirable to reduce consumption of on-board resources during that time and somehow put the crew members "at sleep". Such behaviour can be observed in many hot-blooded animals including mammals, i.e. animals related to humans, which hibernate in order to minimize energy consumption during times of reduced activity and food availability, i.e. winter. While poikilothermic (cold-blooded) animals such as fish or insects constantly adjust their body temperature to the ambient temperature, homoeothermic (warm-blooded) ones such as mammals have to actively enter a state of reduced metabolism. This ability can be observed in different species belonging to different families.
>
> If put into a hypometabolic state, humans would require less energy and food, they would

produce less "waste", use less space, possibly face less emotional stress due to not being consciously faced with isolation, and finally could encounter a far reduced degradation in physical performance than is usually observed during long times of inactivity. Furthermore, the reduced ventilation, heart rate, kidney filtration and CNS activity could make the organism less sensitive to the deleterious effects of microgravity; the radiation effects are expected to be left unchanged instead. If the positive effects of using hypometabolic states appear obvious, there are still several difficulties to be understood better and mastered. One of the big open challenges is to artificially induce hypometabolic states in beings that don't naturally enter into them.

That's the tricky bit. And as Vlad tells me he reminds his colleagues at the European Space Agency, coming out of hibernation could be more dangerous than entering it. The change in heart rate alone could cause intense shock.

He hopes that his Siberian mice might have some of the answers. The main factor to trigger hibernation is not actually the cold but darkness. Temperature is a close second. In Siberia, it is very hot in summer and very cold in winter. He tests the response in his mice by switching laboratory conditions from a very long sixteen-hour day to a shorter eight-hour day. Vlad is watching out for the trigger change in the metabolic rate. He knows their body temperature will drop but the key is saving energy.

Torpor is not the same condition as sleep but sleep is the gateway to it. Mammals enter into hibernation through sleep and they sleep more deeply coming out of it. Vlad is fascinated by patterns of sleep. A study on European starlings found that they slept for five more hours each day in winter than in summer. Birds, like the rest of us, suffer from light pollution. Bats sleep almost continually. I am feeling sore about this because the parish council in our village in Norfolk is proposing to instal high-wattage floodlighting at the football pitch next to my garden. I think of the owls and the bats and the pond creatures and Peggy, wherever she is. A neighbour comes to commiserate; he has moved to the village after suffering a brain tumour and says the natural rhythm of the day and night is a great consolation of country life. He asks: "Will we still see the stars?"

But back to Siberian mice. Vlad says that when exposed to longer hours of darkness, his rodents move from sleep to profound loss of consciousness, which resembles a coma. The rodents' heart rate goes down, from five to seven times a second to just once a second, their brain activity almost flattens and their neurons become less active. It is more like anaesthesia. One question is whether this state can respond to outside influences. If there were, say, a fire in the forest, would hibernating creatures be aware of the danger? The conscious and the unconscious. The sleeping and the waking. The living and the dead.

Vlad emails me after our Zoom meeting with academic links to space missions and neuroscientific research on brain function post cardiac arrests. He signs off: "Good luck with your hedgehog project!"

I can see our tasks are a little unequal in gravity (or perhaps not, since his is in space) but my spirits are lifting at the prospect of my next hedgehog instalment. I am off to Alderney, to find the famous blonde hedgehogs as they come out of hibernation. The Alderney hedgehogs breed a little earlier than those in the colder climate of the UK and I know they are deserving of interest because they have been the subject of study by the venerated naturalist Pat Morris. I find his research in an academic zoological journal and copy down his conclusions:

> In 1989 a questionnaire in Alderney contained references to "fawn hedgehogs", known scientifically as leucistic [which comes from the Greek *leukos*, meaning "white" and refers to the loss of pigmentation in an animal] and identifiable for their creamy white spines, black eyes and pink skins. Sixty-seven per cent of residents who took part in the survey reported sightings of these blond hedgehogs. A further appealing characteristic was that none of the 67 hedgehogs sighted carried fleas. This suggested that the hedgehogs had been transported to the island, because they would have to be flea free to get entry. The discussion was this: leucistic hedgehogs

are very uncommon on the British mainland. There are no predatory mammals in Alderney (immigration policies are as strict for animals as for humans) so paleness is not a survival strategy. Why are they blond?

The report concludes that the genetic basis for colouration in hedgehogs is not known, but the leucistic character may be controlled by a rare recessive gene:

This is consistent with the observed facts: it is rarely manifest on the mainland and none of the reported introductions to Alderney were other than normal coloured. But if one of them carried the gene, and there was a back-cross mating between the F1 (the first filial) generation and the parent, very likely in a small founder population, this would result in 25 per cent leucistic offspring, exactly the proportion evident today. The patchiness and abundance of leucistic animals in the population might facilitate inbreeding, helping to sustain this high prevalence.

With a confined population, free of predators, this situation might continue, but if there are further introductions, or the genetic basis for spine colouration is more complex, the proportion of leucistic animals may well decline. The purpose of this note is to record the present situation.

The small plane bounces onto the landing strip,

surrounded by rugs of yellow gorse and fortifications across the coastline. This was a Victorian naval outpost against the French before it was occupied by the Germans during the Second World War, so visitors tend to combine interests in birds and bunkers. A bracing wind buffets our taxi as we drive up narrow cobbled streets past pastel-coloured houses to the centre of St Anne's, the island's only town.

There is an old-fashioned high street with accountants, lawyers, the Salvation Army, the Rotary Club and old governor-style buildings, along with charity shops and wool shops and a boutique hotel called The Blonde Hedgehog. The post boxes are blue here, and there is a clack of walking sticks on the narrow pavements overrun by men in blazers looking slightly like Stanley Johnson, father of the Prime Minister. Chattering puffin watchers stand around exchanging news of recent sightings. The church, erected by the Hon Canon of Winchester, is surrounded by primroses. I feel as if I am in the middle of a Channel 5 Sunday night thriller. There never seem to be more than about twenty people about, although the population is actually around 2,000.

Alderney's political history is also its natural history. From Roman outpost to Nazi stronghold, it has been occupied and fortified. Its population was evacuated during the Second World War, and forced labour imported. Some fortresses are now *Succession*-style private houses, but most are in ruins. And in this windswept, rocky landscape nature has taken hold. A colony of swallows has arrived. Gulls and puffins and gannets nest among the rocky outposts. There are wildflowers and insects everywhere; indeed there are more species of moths in Alderney than anywhere else in the British Isles .

The coastal path is bright with thrift and sea lavender and rock rose, and sweet-smelling alyssum cascades behind dry-stone walls.

The head of the Alderney Wildlife Trust is a quietly spoken, red-bearded, Viking-featured man in his forties called Roland Gauvain. His family were among the Second World War diaspora of Alderney and he travels between the island and Poole harbour in his sailing boat. He shows a particular tenderness for gulls, which he thinks are often political scapegoats. He is pro the hedgehogs, which he calls "charismatic and cute", but not blind to their peccadilloes. His top-notch night camera traps have caught them biffing each other into roads. He has evidence of them loitering around the eggs of the ground-nesting ringed plovers, and even chasing down a chick.

In between doing his more scientific ecological work, Roland conducts hedgehog and bat walks for visitors. Since lockdown, there has been a surge in nature tourism which he puts down to "perspective". The nature blockbusters of Alderney are the puffins and the blonde hedgehogs. Roland prefers the scientific name leucistic, but the shops and restaurants know what nature tourists like.

Blonde hedgehog table mats and door stops, the Blonde Hedgehog Hotel... Roland tries to direct the producers of nature programmes towards the wonders of the sea caves; he would like hedgehogs to be the shop window for the subtler treasures of nature, the flora and fauna, the extraordinary fungi, but he is realistic about the crowd pleasers.

The anecdotal history of the blonde hedgehogs is slightly awkward. As Pat Morris noted in his study, there is no mention of them before 1960. They were almost certainly imported from Europe. According to island folklore, they arrived in a Harrods bag. The department store did indeed sell animals, including lions, cubs and alligators, before the 1976 Endangered Species Act. It certainly sold hedgehogs. So it is likely that the European hedgehogs arrived in Alderney as pets and then around twenty generations of inbreeding produced the recessive leucistic gene. I like the notion that Harrods hedgehogs are too posh for fleas. They are not at the mercy of badgers because Alderney folk control the animal populations as they choose. So, undeterred by natural predators, the Alderney hedgehogs shimmer across the island, with their palomino-coloured cream and gold spikes.

Kim and I spend the day touring the island – a grand way of describing a 6km walk – and see swallows playing by the cliffs, larks flying high above the gorse and gannets perching on the rocks, which are white with their guano.

In St Anne's are plaques to famous inhabitants. A tall white house in a central square was once lived in by the writer of Arthurian legend, T.H. White. His book, *The*

Once and Future King, is about the natural world, and has a memorable description of woodland at nightfall, of sleeping outdoors:

> The boy [Wart] slept well in the woodland nest where he had laid himself down, in that kind of thin but refreshing sleep which people have when they begin to lie out of doors. At first he only dipped below the surface of sleep, and skimmed along like a salmon in shallow water, so close to the surface that he fancied himself in the air. He thought himself awake when he was already asleep. He saw the stars above his face, whirling on their silent and sleepless axes and the leaves of the trees rustling against them and he heard small changes in the grass.

After Wart – who grows up to be King Arthur and challenges the brutal basis of war that might is right, with a new code of chivalry – meets Merlyn the wizard, he learns to swim as a fish and to fly with the wild geese. Wart is lifted from the water meadows by the wind:

> In this enormous flatness, there lived one element – the wind. For it was an element. It was a dimension, a power of darkness... Horizontal, soundless except for a peculiar boom, tangible, infinite, the astounding dimensional weight of it streamed across the mud... The Wart, facing into this wind, felt that he was uncreated. Except for the wet solid-

ity under his webbed feet, he was living in nothing – a solid nothing, like chaos.

The ascension and flight of the geese is a kind of purgatory until they reach the "huge remorseless sea". I think of my father's description of watching the pink-footed geese take off in their thousands and of the metaphor of death it became when I read the passage, to the music of Sibelius's "Swan" theme, at his funeral.

But T.H. White goes on to make the boy-goose's flight, beyond the darkness, glorious.

"The dawn, the sea dawn and the mastery of ordered flight were of such intense beauty that the boy was moved to sing. He wanted to cry a chorus to life, and, since a thousand geese were on the wing about him, he had not long to wait."

In T.H. White's world, the geese may be metaphysical, but hedgehogs are there to be eaten. Wart is turned into a badger and fiercely threatens a hedgehog trying to sleep in a bed of leaves.

"The more you squeal," said the Wart, "the more I shall gnash. It makes my blood boil within me."

"Ah, Measter Brock," cried the hedgehog, holding himself tight shut. "Good Measter Brock, show mercy to a poor urchin and don't 'ee be tyrannical. Us be'nt no common tiggy, measter, for to be munched and mumbled. Have mercy, kind sir, on a harmless fleabitten crofter which can't tell his left hand nor his right."

The image of the hedgehog takes quite a dent from Alderney's most famous writer. I wonder if White, who died in 1964, was a little behind Pat Morris in his knowledge of developments in the natural world. Perhaps he had never seen or heard of the blonde hedgehogs of Alderney.

I cannot believe that creatures possessing such knockout glamour would be obsequious and silly. Beauty bestows self-containment. And I am anxious to see one of these showstoppers. It is impossible to give an accurate number for the blonde hedgehog population, although tracking is underway. But there are several hundred of them.

A group of about twelve show-goers, in thick jumpers and anoraks, meet at the Alderney Wildlife Trust offices at 8pm for our bat and hedgehog walk. One couple have pictures on their phone of the hedgehog they have rescued and look after at their home in Wales. I look at it enviously, wondering again, where on earth is Peggy? Then we follow Roland to the churchyard to look first off for the pipistrelle bat. We wave frequency locators above our heads to try to pick up their cries. Roland asks fun fact questions to keep our attention while we wait. "What other flying mammals are there besides bats?" One of our party calls out: "Flying squirrels!" "Wrong! They can only glide for short distances."

We wait a bit longer. Last week was warmer and this patch of ground turned into a Countryfile spring special, but it is chilly again now and the bats and hedgehogs have gone quiet. One lady fills the silence with an indignant monologue about the lack of cat licences when you see the damage they can cause to wildlife. She falters: "I don't want to offend anyone..."

Suddenly, our machines are calling and a delicate pipistrelle bat flies, limbs stretched and cloaked, close above our heads. Then more. We, the anoraks, beam at each other in the darkness. Then we file after Roland again, out of the churchyard, up and down side streets, across the cricket pitch. He talks a little more about the leucistics. You would have thought their colouring would put them at an evolutionary disadvantage for they lack camouflage, he says, but it at least makes them more visible on the roads.

We are peering over stone walls and scanning verges and watching our feet. We must look like a troupe of out-of-season carol singers. Finally, Ronald leads us down a driveway and into someone's back garden. The house belongs to a hedgehog volunteer and he knows there is a feeding station there. He goes ahead and flashes a torch back to us. We creep across the lawn in the shadows... and there in the spotlight is the Marilyn Monroe of hedgehogs, voluptuously blonde, tripping daintily in front of the brick terrace before disappearing again into the darkness. I see her for a minute and it is worth every second. The winter is truly over and the show must go on.

10

FRIENDS AND ENEMIES: BADGERS, DOGS AND HUMANS

"Well, it's time we were all in bed," said the Badger, getting up and fetching flat candlesticks.

"Come along, you two, and I'll show you your quarters. And take your time tomorrow morning – breakfast at any hour you please!"

He conducted the two animals to a long room that seemed half bedchamber and half loft. The Badger's winter stores, which indeed were visible everywhere, took up half the room... but the two little white beds on the remainder of the floor looked soft and inviting, and the linen on them, though coarse, was clean and smelt beautifully of lavender; and the Mole and the Water Rat, shaking off their garments in some thirty seconds, tumbled in between the sheets in great joy and contentment.

In accordance with the kindly Badger's injunctions, the two tired animals came down to breakfast very late next morning, and found a bright fire burning in the kitchen, and two young hedgehogs sitting on a bench at the table, eating oatmeal porridge out of wooden bowls. The hedgehogs dropped their spoons, rose to their feet and ducked their heads respectfully as the two entered.

"There, sit down, sit down," said the Rat pleasantly, "and go on with your porridge. Where have you come from? Lost your way in the snow, I suppose?"

"Yes, please, sir," said the elder of the two hedgehogs respectfully. "Me and little Billy here, we was trying to find our way to school – mother would have us go, was the weather ever so – and of course we lost ourselves, sir, and Billy he got frightened and took and cried, being young and fainthearted. And at last we happened up against Mr Badger's back door and made so bold as to knock, sir, for Mr Badger he's a kind-hearted gentleman, as everyone knows…"

This is the literary expression of a patriotic vision of English wildlife, so deeply felt by Stephanie from the Natural History Museum, by Hugh Warwick and by all those who care about hedgehogs. It is a story of home and hearth, of bacon for breakfast and afternoon buttered toast by the fire and hierarchies of native wildlife, with badgers as the respected Rotary Club-style patriarchs. Hmm. But what would actually have happened if a couple of juvenile hedgehogs had shown up at a badger's home during the hibernation months? Would they have been given porridge? Or been flipped and disinterred?

T.H. White is probably truer: "Badgers are one of the few creatures which can munch up hedgehogs unconcernedly, just as they can munch up everything else from wasp's nests to baby rabbits."

Odd, then, that in my list of qualifications to release Peggy back into the wild, I was not asked about neighbouring badgers. I was asked about my habitat and my humanity, and if I owned a dog. Lockdown has made us a country of dog owners again.

Although spikes are of course a deterrent for soft curious noses, dogs can bark and circle and chase hedgehogs and generally make nuisances of themselves. But this doesn't seem to preclude the two of them from becoming friends.

My hedgehog-loving friend Jane Byam Shaw told me that she had read about dogs in Wales trained to find and protect hedgehogs. And so it was that I drove to Wrexham, in the verdant Welsh hills, to meet Henry, a springer spaniel hedgehog detection dog and his handler Louise Wilson.

Both are forces of nature. Louise, aged 40, is warm, sexy, fearless and blonde with a throaty Wigan accent. She seems to belong outside but we get to sit on an upper floor of a barn to watch the corporate presentation of her detection agency K9. She has a diploma from Chester University in animal behaviour, and has found a market opportunity handling detection dogs for drugs and explosives. Her CV includes war zones and HM Revenue and Customs. Hers is a world of scents, but these days it is more likely to be otter poo than heroin.

Henry, the hedgehog finder, also has an unusual biography. He was kicked out of five homes before Louise found him in the rescue centre. You need particular qualities to be a detection dog. Dogs, like children, are generally encouraged to be obedient and well mannered. But Louise, and her easy-going partner, Kevin, say they "allow them to be dogs". Louise wants energy, dynamism, curiosity, intelligence. "We look for wilful disobedience."

Most interesting, in their most dog-like incarnations, they are not predatory. Some breeds are more suited for the work than others. Springer and cocker Spaniels and Labradors score highly, except for chocolate Labradors, which are genetically altered and thus less "dog-like". The same goes for the fancy breeds favoured in lockdown. "Cockapoo?" Kevin sighs, arms folded.

Louise shows me a slide of a very dog-like spaniel climbing over their kitchen cupboards and she smiles indulgently. When her six-year-old son complains that one of their twelve dogs has destroyed one of his toys, she asks him what he expects if he leaves his toys lying around.

When I meet Henry, he has an exuberance bordering on the maniacal. Louise can barely hold him on the lead, which she says is one of his virtues. When she lets him off, he bounds across the training centre of benches, bales of hay and various assault course objects. But it is not purposeless high spirits. He is always following his nose. There are two boxes on a table containing hedgehog coats and it takes him about ten seconds to stop next to them. Louise says she and Kevin do not bother with commands and Henry does not need them.

And yet, when Henry finds a hedgehog nest, he is gentle and still, merely pointing at it to help the ecologists. Louise's move from weapons, drugs or "clandestines", by which she means stowaways, to natural wildlife, while running her detection agency has opened up a new world of smells and other clues. While she was accepted as an equal when she worked with the police or armed forces, ecologists were more suspicious of her because of her lack of academic qualifications. Like Beatrix Potter, she proved herself. She is, these days, content to push a springer spaniel on a paddle board down muddy rivers in search of river life. Kevin, meanwhile, has a good line in rats and bats. He was the Pied Piper of the *Sir David Attenborough* research vessel before it sailed for the Antarctic. Nowadays, he is checking the impact that the expansion of wind turbines is having across the country on bats. The wildlife on Louise and Kevin's list grows longer: great crested newts, pine martins, and globally, cheetahs, elephants, wolves, bears. "To be honest, though," she says dreamily. "I really want to work with chimpanzees."

Meanwhile, Louise has become fond of the homes of dormice and voles, which are neatly laid out, with ramps and woven sleeping quarters. Her vole detection dog, Hettie, often finds voles by sniffing out their self-made feeding stations that look peacefully out at the sunset.

Henry turned out to be perfectly suited for hedgehogs. He needs some space, and hedgehogs cover large areas. There is no point in putting Henry in small rooms or containers, looking for explosives. He is also trained to expect rewards, in particular his favourite ball. The dogs trained to detect bombs and explosives cannot canter about expecting rewards – they need to be more temperamentally self-contained.

Henry is also unfussed by the stink of hedgehogs and the fleas that tend to settle around them. Louise is proud of his ability to find the poo of endangered species. "The perfect poo, fresh, fresh, fresh."

He is as content searching at night as he is during the day. His sense of smell is a 100,000 times more sensitive than that of a human.

It is a subtle, complex environment. The thing about drugs and explosives is that they are out of context with their surroundings. But hedgehogs are part of a rich and wondrous ecosystem. There will be many scents nearby, all of which belong there. I ask about the presence of badgers: "Badgers are only a threat if they have been chased out of their habitat," she says stoutly.

If humans allow room for nature, everything can co-exist. Whether or not it is thanks to Henry, the hedgehog population in their part of Wales is rising. The population census largely depends on roadkill, and they see plenty of hedgehogs flattened on hilly routes.

Zac Goldsmith shares Louise's view of the relationship between the hedgehog and the badger. When we are fighting over the same resources, relationships break down. He reflects on the balance: "We know if you have a big proportion of badgers in an area, there are fewer hedgehogs, all other things being equal, ground cover, food to sustain all populations, a balanced population. We haven't suddenly introduced badgers into the UK countryside and I don't know what the population of badgers is but the hedgehog population has collapsed and it has not collapsed in proportion to the rise in badgers. In a bleak landscape dominated by badgers, you are not going to have hedgehogs but the answer is not to get rid of badgers.

"There is nothing new about having dry periods, maybe they have become more extreme but nature has been dealing with this stuff for ever. If you look after soil, vegetation, trees, you will hold onto moisture longer than in mono grass. Those changes that are happening to hedgehogs would be better served with a healthy ecosystem."

How should we do that?

Zac mentions again the transformative action of the

hedgehog-nurturing jeweller in Barnes, and so I decide to go and find him. I settle at a window table in the Rocks Lane café and look out at a cricket match, played in damp whites. I am looking out for an eccentric. But then, through the drizzle, a debonair figure in linen comes through the door. Only on his jacket is a little giveaway, a hedgehog badge.

How has a gemmologist, who sells diamonds worth millions to the world's oligarchs, become so besotted by hedgehogs? Michel, now in his sixties, lays out his life. A childhood in the Belgian Congo, where his parents had a coffee plantation, and after the country's independence in 1960, educated by nuns in Montreal. He then trained as a gemmologist, because it might lead him to life's prizes, "cash and women". Diamonds have a universal currency as a means of seduction.

He came to the UK in the 1980s and settled here with a British wife. The second time he fell in love was when his dog unearthed a hedgehog in his garden in Barnes about ten years ago. He was both infatuated and indignant that hedgehogs were not more protected and celebrated.

He asks, "Why are they not on stamps? They should be our national symbol."

He thought of what he could do and realised that holes in fences and walls would save the hedgehogs. So he knocked on the doors of his neighbours, and, being a merchant by nature and having an artistic eye, he put up posters and made hedgehog pins to rouse Barnes village into action.

"Some people kept the posters," he says with casual pride.

His offer was that he would drill for free, and he persuaded his electrician to help him. Together, they made a thousand hedgehog holes.

The great liberation of Barnes has saved the hedgehog population, but Michel says that it is a two-way (hedgehog) street. "It also saved my mind," he says.

With his day job of selling millions of pounds of jewels, including to Russian satellite states, he felt he was selling his soul. It was hedgehogs, he says, "that changed my view of humanity". His soul was regained.

In practical terms, he makes holes for hedgehogs. Philosophically, he says, he is trying to "create a union between hedgehogs and humankind".

And this union happens. There's a local King's Counsel in Barnes who sometimes phones him, desolate, at 11pm because his hedgehogs have not appeared at their feeding station. The appearance of the hedgehogs has become the verdict on his way of life.

Michel has witnessed in his travelled life that humankind finds it easier to embrace emotion when it does not involve personal sacrifice or inconvenience. Why does everyone love Mrs Tiggy-Winkle, but then replace their gardens with plastic grass? he asks. The particular, the here and now, matters as much as the general good.

He tells me a sad story about his father, an Auschwitz survivor, who had his number carved into his arm. When he was 90, he moved into a nursing home, and not one person there asked him about the number. "Everyone knows about Auschwitz, people travel there to see it. But they do not care about the man in the home. He was just an old man dying."

Only connect. Michel talks about the puzzle of humankind and nature and the danger of removing a key piece. The hedgehog. "People have to take responsibility. I have to find a way of connecting hedgehogs to human beings. Really, it is all I want."

Somehow, we have to make humanity feel that it is part of the natural world, not an invader of it. I think of the burial service in *The Book of Common Prayer*. "We therefore commit this body to the ground, earth to earth, ashes to ashes, dust to dust; in sure and certain hope of the Resurrection to eternal life."

Two days later I return home, and in the garden of the house where my grandson Billy lives with his parents, my son Henry and his wife Anna, nearby in Norfolk, we scatter my dad's ashes in a place he loved, under a tree in which stone curlews had nested.

The family live on the edge of Ministry of Defence land, which means that the ground is undeveloped and nature is left in peace. There are trout and otters in the chalk stream, and among the rustling trees the birds chatter as if it is school playtime.

Under a tulip tree of citrus-coloured fresh leaves, encircled by bluebells and wild grasses, my son and Billy dig a hole and we scatter Noel's ashes, the texture of coarse grey sand, into it, along with sprigs of rosemary for remembrance. My brother lights a candle, which continues to burn to its quick despite the soft rain and sudden breezes.

A few times it flickers but it never gives up. I wonder if it was a flame such as this that my father saw when he passed from life to death.

After we finish scattering the ashes, we hear above us the familiar haunting cry of wild geese and a line of three flap over us. A fly-past. Truly, we commit this body to the ground. My father's faith was that nature was an embodiment of the divine, and here he is as part of Creation, earth to earth.

11

WAR AND PEACE

My former BBC colleague Frank Gardner is on the *Today* programme talking about military exercises that Estonia is conducting to protect itself and other small neighbouring countries from Russian aggression. The drill is called "Operation Hedgehog". Frank says it seems a cosy name for a show of weapons, but then that is the appeal.

I know now why I am so sympathetic towards hedgehogs. They are a symbol of Nato for good reason: they are resourceful and self-reliant and peaceful – though defensive if challenged. Their numbers are small but they do not give up. They are survivors.

There is also a natural European alliance of hedgehogs. The UK hedgehog is the same as the European hedgehog and the countries that are fond of hedgehogs tend to share other values.

In the Integrated Review of Security, Defence, Development and Foreign Policy, the soon-to-be deposed Prime Minister Johnson states the position of the UK: "We will be open to the world, free to tread our own path, blessed with a global network of friends and partners." It sounds like a world made for hedgehogs.

Meanwhile, in Ukraine, there are voluntary patrols in Irpin, a commuter town on the outskirts of Kyiv. When Moscow launched its assault, neighbours banded together with any weapons they could find. The nicknames of the men include Hulk, Doberman and Beard. They call their ad hoc unit the Hedgehogs, because of their strategy of making their neighbourhood too difficult for the Russians to touch.

The Hedgehogs are now training to go to the East with the local Territorial Defence forces. Hulk says: "We are defending our land. It's important that we didn't go to anyone else's country. They came here and they are killing our women and children. So we are ready to fight and defend to the last one of us."

The question we ask under our breaths is: are those brave hedgehogs units capable of winning?

The Hedgehog Diaries

In his book, *The Hedgehog, the Fox and The Magister's Pox*, Stephen Jay Gould calls for reconciliation rather than dichotomies. The fox AND the hedgehog. But if you have to pick one, the hedgehog has the advantage, because of its moral compass in times of peril. The fox is wily, but is often captured, for instance in a hunt. The hedgehog is more likely to be unscathed. "If we roll with the punches, maintain the guts of our inner integrity and keep our prickles high, we can't lose," according to Gould.

In the case of Russia and Ukraine, it is not a fox but a bear in relative contrast to a hedgehog and I pray that it is enough for the hedgehog to frown and roll up into a ball. Defensive, but never the aggressor. As Hulk said: "We didn't go to anyone else's country."

I look up on YouTube a 1975 Soviet animated film called *Hedgehog in the Fog*. The plot line is fairy tale and geopolitical. The hedgehog sets off for his evening visit to his friend the bear cub. Every evening the two meet to have tea and count the stars. This evening, the hedgehog is bringing the bear cub some raspberry jam as a treat. As he walks through the woods, the hedgehog sees a beautiful white horse which then disappears into heavy fog. Curious, the hedgehog starts to explore the fog and loses his way. After some dream-like sequences, the hedgehog runs into the bear cub who has been searching for him. The two friends sit by the fire and drink tea looking at the stars.

No one expects the war to end with the bear and the hedgehog sitting by the fire and drinking tea. I think back to visiting the Beatrix Potter exhibition at the Victoria and Albert Museum on the day that Putin unleashed his war on Ukraine and days after my dad died. It was as if darkness had descended on the world.

The remaking of private and public worlds has to start somewhere.

The hedgehog is the metaphor chosen by philosophers. It is a Trojan horse for the British national treasure Hugh Warwick, whom I had met through Jane Byam-Shaw. As you may have gathered, Hugh – author, stand-up, social media star – is a life-long friend to hedgehogs. He lives the hedgehog values espoused by Rowan Williams. He looks slightly like a hobbit, friendly, muscular and stout with soft brown-grey facial hair.

His house and garden on the outskirts of Oxford have den-like qualities, piles of books, an array of flower pots. Despite his living commitment to hedgehogs, none visit this garden. The house happens to be part of a wider stretch of city planning that does not suit hedgehogs.

Hugh, an ecologist, has strong views on how society could function better if it paid attention to nature but he does not preach. He has learned that a chat about hedgehogs is more effective. He has been on protests where security guards are disarmed, emotionally if not physically, by some fun hedgehog facts.

At parties, strangers are always happy to talk to him about hedgehogs. After all, the hedgehog is unfailingly voted the nation's favourite animal. Hugh says: "They are so British. We don't like our neighbours particularly, preferring to be on our own. We would love to get to sleep for the whole winter. Imagine the environmental benefits of shutting down?"

He also does a hedgehog comedy sketch, which is more revolution by stealth. His soapboxes are Women's Institutes events, or Probus Clubs. He does not need to mention politics. He just describes the lives of hedgehogs: their peaceful co-existence with humans, their ancient heritage, they way they link countryside and suburbia, garden and field. Only connect.

The emotional tug of hedgehogs is bound up with memories of childhood.

Hugh reckons that hedgehogs are the most common wild animal to be mentioned in children's books, and older adults remember when hedgehogs were among us. He says: "They are cute, a little bit silly, and unusual, the only spinal mammal in the UK. You use something small to tell a bigger story."

The bigger story has been that a hedgehog-friendly environment is a sign of a harmony with nature, while their absence speaks of a land out of joint.

Hugh acknowledges, for instance, that badger populations have increased in places where hedgehogs would naturally thrive, such as the South-West of England. If badgers cannot find their own sources of food, they move into the territory of hedgehogs. And we know that frowning and curling up into a ball is no defence against badgers.

But Hugh is using hedgehogs now for a different motive, one of rational realism. Like Stephen Jay Gould, he is tired of polarities and dichotomies and special interests. Thus, the great patron of hedgehogs is prepared to say that sometimes it is necessary to kill hedgehogs in the interest of the greater good.

The famous example is the Orkneys. You can love hedgehogs until they attack the eggs – and chicks – of Arctic terns. As it happened, the subject of Hugh Warwick's 1986 degree project was counting hedgehogs and the effect they had on birds on the Orkney islands. This was the beginning of his life's work of making a world fit for hedgehogs, and it included recognising Darwinian conflicts and principles of co-existence.

In 2004, a culling of hedgehogs in the Hebrides caught the imagination of the media, and Hugh found that his own research was being cited by the cullists as supporting evidence, although in fact this was not what Hugh had advocated – or at least not for the UK, where he favoured enforced migration. "It wasn't a problem of science but of communication," he says ruefully.

His next book will not be a heartwarming read about hedgehogs, like his first one, *A Prickly Affair*. It will be a big, difficult book about the complexity of ecology. It will be head over heart.

I am still trying to find that balance. I had not expected the incredulity of loss, my inability to tell my dad about all these naturalist arguments, which he would have so much enjoyed. A lifetime of conversation becomes a monologue.

Meanwhile, I have lost my value as a consumer. The usual retail marketing of Father's Day falters as gift companies send me messages asking if I would prefer not to hear from them. Someone whose online history includes coffins must alarm data harvesters.

My mother cannot yet bring herself to return to the home that she shared with my father. Everything is exactly as it was the day he left hospital and they arrived together at the nursing home. By my father's chair is his pile of books, with postcards from old friends as bookmarks. The books are a mix of poetry, and the other kinds of titles he liked. *Ships of Heaven*, by Christopher Somerville, *Last Days in Old Europe*, by Richard Bassett, *Gather the Fragments*, by Alan Ecclestone.

There are a few political and historical hardbacks that I had bought him and suspect he did not finish. And books published now that he will never start, Antony Beevor's book on Russia primary among them.

Meanwhile, in his study, there are laborious lists for Waitrose orders that Kim and I used to process each week. We would roll our eyes over his frugality – "one carrot, one grapefruit" – and his generational expectation of puddings – "raspberry sponge, dairy toffees". His writing resembled musical notes with quaver-like squiggles and double bar lines. He wrote everything down, particularly nearing the end. On his Roberts Radio was a post-it reminder: R3 91:95 R4, 94.0. His decline addressed with lists and perseverance.

Usually, we would have taken him and my mother to Cornwall in the summer, but nobody talks of that now. Instead, Kim and I go to the Hebrides because packing our binoculars and going to look at birds is the best tribute to him I can think of. Just because I can't see him, doesn't mean that he isn't there.

The Sound of Mull is charcoal-grey and choppy. It is submarine territory, dark and deep and lethal. We head out on a boat trip to look at porpoises, but the North Atlantic swell is too great and so we turn back. What catches the skipper's eye instead is the shape perched in and partly camouflaged by the Scottish pines. It reveals itself only when it lifts its enormous wings and glides down to the level of the gulls; it is a Scottish sea eagle. The magnificent bird acts as a drone and it takes what it sees. The forest floors and cliff ledges are strewn with skeletons of small mammals, including, I am sorry to say, hedgehogs.

War and peace, life and death must co-exist. A peeling, friendly-looking rowing boat moored up at Craignure, Mull, is called *Lethal Weapon*, named before Russia familiarised us all with type-54 pistols, sub-machine guns, assault rifles, grenade launchers, flame throwers, self-propelled mortars and tanks.

On this island of ferns, waterfalls, eagles and otters, and Mendelssohn's overture, nature's order prevails. We head out to look at Iona, where the boulders of rain clouds lift to reveal the Abbey. The first monks headed out here from Ireland in the sixth century, bearing their high Celtic crosses and led by Columba, who lived on the island till his death, practising perseverance: "...for the place where his bones rest is still visited by the light of heaven and by numbers of angels."

In the doorway of the West Range of Iona Abbey is a swallow's nest. Parents fly in and out, ignoring human bystanders. The crack in the wall is home and the chicks are merrily insatiable.

It is a peaceful place, a spiritual retreat for those of all faiths or none. Even the storm of politics is quiet here. As the squall envelops Westminster with mass Cabinet resignations in protest over the Prime Minister's chaotic administration and persistent untruths, I go to visit the grave of John Smith, the Scottish Labour leader and perhaps a great loss as a possible Prime Minister, who died of a heart attack in 1994, aged 56.

The message on the plain boulder on the grass, near the abbey, is an expression of probity; thin, gold monastic letters read: "An honest man's the noblest work of God."

John Smith's achievement in the end was honesty rather than hectic drama. A hedgehog rather than a fox. It is far from Westminster where Boris Johnson fights on in Roman style, dedicated to the heroic view of political history. And yet, Boris understands the philosophical truth of the futility of ambition, saying at one point during his trial by committee, "all flesh is grass".

The following day he resigns, observing: "The herd is powerful and when it moves, it moves."

He is evoking the African plains and river crossings and himself as one of the big beasts. Predators come in different forms, often human.

From Iona, we take a ferry to the island of Uist, where my unheroic mission is to follow in Hugh Warwick's footsteps, and find out whether hedgehogs should always prevail or whether they too must submit to a greater design of Creation.

The repatriation of the hedgehogs to the mainland has not been entirely successful but it is continuing. The Darwinian struggle for survival, sardonically observed by Boris Johnson in Westminster, is literal here.

Introducing a species without an ecosystem of predators causes mayhem. Even the lovely sea eagles here are regarded warily by the crofters, who seek compensation for any lambs that disappear as a result. The protection of buzzards means that the eagles need more to eat.

If you are a vole or a meadow pipit your expectations of survival are small. Nobody is rushing to save the eels from otters; the otters on the west coast of Scotland have benefited from *Ring of Bright Water* by Gavin Maxwell, just as badgers can thank *The Wind in the Willows* and hedgehogs *Mrs Tiggy-Winkle*.

But not even Mrs Tiggy-Winkle can win over the naturalists of the Uists and Barra, where the gull chicks were terrorised by the hedgehogs. Who came first, the hedgehog or the egg? Our Uist guide claims that hedgehogs were imported by a gardener exasperated by slugs. The rest is Darwin.

In Alderney, it was hedgehogs' harassment of ground-nesting plovers, taking eggs and sometimes chicks, that earned them the disapprobation of environmentalists. In Uist, it is the fate of the waders.

Watching a flock of Arctic terns pass, pristine and balletic over the white sand of a North Uist beach, I see why you would wish to save them. The birds have the longest migratory path of any bird, coming from the Antarctic coast to breed here. The least we can do is keep the eggs safe.

The complexity of ecology, or Creation, is hard to fathom but awesome to observe. I am starting to learn the elementary rule of nature watching, which is patience and serendipity. An otter disappears behind a seaweed-covered rock but then half an hour later returns to roll on its back, flattening its waterlogged fur in full sight.

I happen to look round and see a short-eared owl staring back at me. We scan the hill tops for eagles but see nothing. They are not visible but they are there.

If I imagine my father, he is holding up a pair of binoculars. He absorbed nature and now is absorbed by nature, as for all of us flesh is grass. I am no longer mourning, but watching the natural world. And I remember the Bidding Prayer for "all those who rejoice with us, but upon another shore and in a greater light…"

We return to Norfolk in scorching temperatures – an accelerated climate that is bad news for hedgehogs in general. But for me there is a patch of deepest contentment. By the pond is a dark, round shape. It is a hedgehog. For this moment, all is right with the world.

With thanks to the brilliant Aurea Carpenter and Rebecca Nicolson for taking me with them on their exciting new publishing venture, and to all the hedgehog warriors I interviewed for this book. And with admiration for the courage of my shyly observant mother, Susan Harvey, for learning to live without the protection of her life's partner.